CW00323210

To renew this book, phone 0845 1202811 or visit
our website at www.libcat.oxfordshire.gov.uk
You will need your library PIN number
(available from your library)

OXFORDSHIRE
COUNTY COUNCIL
SOCIAL & COMMUNITY SERVICES
www.oxfordshire.gov.uk

Pearson Education Limited
Edinburgh Gate, Harlow,
Essex CM20 2JE, England
and Associated Companies throughout the world.

ISBN: 978-1-4058-8269-9

First published in Great Britain by Faber & Faber 1988
New edition first published by Penguin Books Ltd 2000
This edition first published 2008

1 3 5 7 9 10 8 6 4 2

Original copyright © Kazuo Ishiguro 1988
Text copyright © Pearson Education Ltd 2008

The moral rights of the authors have been asserted

Typeset by Graphicraft Ltd, Hong Kong
Set in 11/14pt Bembo
Printed in China
SWTC/01

For a complete list of the titles available in the Penguin Readers series please write to your local
Pearson Longman office or to: Penguin Readers Marketing Department, Pearson Education,
Edinburgh Gate, Harlow, Essex CM20 2JE, England.

Contents

Introduction

'It's wrong that a man can't explore his own country. Take my advice and get out of the house for a few days.'

As you might expect, I did not accept Mr Farraday's invitation immediately... The change in my attitude to this same suggestion over the following days is mainly due to – and why should I hide it? – the arrival of Miss Kenton's letter.

In the summer of 1956 Mr Farraday, the new, wealthy, American owner of Darlington Hall, encourages his ageing butler, Stevens, to borrow his car and take a well-earned holiday. At first, Stevens politely rejects the offer. He feels that he does not need to travel in order to know his country. It has been his 'privilege to see the best of England over the years' within the walls of Darlington Hall. But then Stevens receives a letter from someone he has not seen for twenty years – Miss Kenton. In the years before World War II, Miss Kenton worked as the housekeeper at Darlington Hall. Twenty years later, she tells Stevens in her letter about her married life. Stevens believes, from the tone of her letter, that her marriage is unhappy, and he begins to think that she may wish to return to Darlington Hall. He therefore decides to accept Mr Farraday's offer of a short holiday, and sets out in his employer's car on a journey that will take him not only into the depths of the English countryside, but also into the depths of his own past.

The Remains of the Day contains an unforgettable description of life between the two world wars in a Great English House. One of the main subjects of the story is the decline of the land-owning English upper classes. In the years before World War II, Lord Darlington is at the height of his powers and influence. Darlington Hall has a staff of twenty-eight people, and important international conferences are held there. The important guests at Darlington Hall include Mr Churchill, Lord Halifax, the German Ambassador (Herr Ribbentrop) and the British Prime Minister (Mr Chamberlain, although his name is never actually mentioned). However, ten years after the war, in 1956, Darlington Hall has a staff of only four people. Lord Darlington is a changed man, hated because of his earlier sympathy for Nazi Germany. The presence of the new owner, Mr Farraday, emphasizes the decline of the English upper classes. Like Mr Lewis, who attends Lord Darlington's conference in 1922 and criticizes Lord Darlington for not understanding the modern world, Mr Farraday is American. After World War II, the British government introduced large tax increases which particularly affected the land-owning upper classes. Many English landowners were unable to leave their property to their children, and wealthy foreigners were therefore the only people who were able to afford large country houses and their lands. One of the underlying meanings of the story's title, *The Remains of the Day*, refers to the 'remains' of old country houses that the English upper classes can no longer afford.

There is, however, another sense of the title. *The Remains of the Day* also refers to evening, which many people think is the best time of the day because then they can think back to their day's work. The evening is symbolic of older age, the period when people can reflect on and assess their whole life. This provides the story with its main subject. During his journey to the West of England to visit Miss Kenton again, Stevens has the opportunity to reconsider his loyalty to Lord Darlington, the importance of dignity in his life, and even his relationship with his father. But, most importantly, he is forced to think about the true nature of his relationship with Miss Kenton. As he remembers past conversations and incidents, he realizes that this relationship with Miss Kenton was more than just a professional relationship between a butler and a housekeeper. Beneath their polite, professional respect for each other, there were deeper feelings which neither of them has been prepared to admit.

The Remains of the Day, therefore, is more than just a story about life in a great English country house. It is a remarkable story of lost causes and a lost love – an inventive, almost magical, story of a man's exploration of his own life, and his heart-breaking attempt to make sense of it.

Kazuo Ishiguro was born in Nagasaki, Japan, in 1954, but has lived in England since he was five. His first novel, *A Pale View of Hills*, was published in 1982. Since then he has written five more novels: *An Artist of the Floating World* (1986), *The Remains of the Day* (1989), *The Unconsoled* (1995), *When We Were Orphans* (2000), and *Never Let Me Go* (2005). *An Artist of the Floating World* won the Whitbread Prize in 1986, and *The Remains of the Day* won the biggest literary prize in England, the Booker Prize. In 2005, Time Magazine released its list of the one hundred greatest books in the English language since the magazine began in 1923. *Never Let Me Go* was the most recently published book on the list.

Apart from his novels, Ishiguro has also written two films: *The Saddest Music in the World* (2003) and *The White Countess* (2005). The famous film makers James Ivory and Ismail Merchant made a very successful film of *The Remains of the Day* in 1993, with Anthony Hopkins as Stevens and Emma Thompson as Miss Kenton.

Chapter 1   Staff Plans

July 1956

It seems increasingly likely that I will undertake the expedition that has been on my mind for some days. It is an expedition which I will undertake alone, in the comfort of Mr Farraday's Ford. It will take me through much of the finest countryside in England to the West Country, and may keep me away from Darlington Hall for five or six days. Mr Farraday himself suggested the idea to me one afternoon almost a fortnight ago, when I was dusting the paintings in the library.

I was, in fact, on the stepladder when my employer entered the room. He was carrying a few books which he presumably wished to return to the shelves. He took the opportunity to inform me that he had arranged to return to the United States for a period of five weeks between August and September. After making this announcement, he put his books down on a table, sat down and stretched his legs. Then he said:

'Stevens, I don't expect you to be locked up here in this house all the time while I'm away. Why don't you take the car and drive off somewhere for a few days?'

This was so unexpected that, at first, I did not quite know how to reply. I certainly thanked him for his consideration, but I probably said nothing very definite, for my employer went on:

'I'm serious, Stevens. I really think you should take a break. I'll pay for the petrol. You fellows, you're always locked up in these big houses. How do you ever manage to see anything of this beautiful country of yours?'

'It has been my privilege to see the best of England over the years, sir, within these walls,' I replied.

Mr Farraday did not seem to understand this statement, for he continued:

'I mean it, Stevens. It's wrong that a man can't explore his own country. Take my advice and get out of the house for a few days.'

As you might expect, I did not accept Mr Farraday's invitation immediately. I regarded it as just another example of an American gentleman's unfamiliarity with English custom. The change in my attitude to this same suggestion over the following days is mainly due to – and why should I hide it? – the arrival of Miss Kenton's letter, her first in almost seven years. But let me make it immediately clear what I mean by this. Miss Kenton's letter gave me an idea concerning professional matters here at Darlington Hall.

Over the past few months, I have been responsible for a series of small errors in the performance of my duties. None of these errors has been at all serious. Nevertheless, I am not accustomed to making errors, and I have found this development rather upsetting. The arrival of Miss Kenton's letter, however, opened my eyes to a simple truth: that these small errors of recent months have been the result of a faulty staff plan.

It is, of course, the responsibility of every butler to take great care when creating a staff plan. I agree with the view that the ability to organize staff duties is central to the skills of a good butler. If, therefore, the present staff plan is at fault, I can only blame myself. However, in my defence, I must say that my task has been unusually difficult.

After purchasing Darlington Hall, Mr Farraday had to remain in the United States for four months. He was, however, keen to keep the staff that had served Lord Darlington so well. This 'staff' was, in fact, only a small team of six people who continued to look after the house for Lord Darlington's relatives until it was sold. I regret that, when the purchase was completed, I could not prevent four of the five other members of staff leaving for new employment. Only Mrs Clements and I remained. I informed my new employer of the situation, and was told to employ more staff.

But, as you know, it is not easy to find satisfactory staff nowadays. By the time Mr Farraday arrived at Darlington Hall, I had only employed two new people. When I told him of my difficulties, Mr Farraday requested a staff plan which would allow the present staff of four to run the house. Parts of the house, he said, might have to be shut down. He was sure, though, that, with my skill and experience, I could keep most of the rooms in use.

There was a time when a staff of twenty-eight had been employed here at Darlington Hall, so I felt, at that moment, a little anxious. Mr Farraday must have noticed the worried look on my face, although I tried to hide it from him, because he added:

'Of course, if it is necessary, you may hire an additional member of staff. But I would be most grateful if you could try working with four.'

I spent many hours on the staff plan. I wanted Mrs Clements to suffer as little change to her routine as possible. The two new young girls, Rosemary and Agnes, were inexperienced, so I could not expect them to do too much. This meant, of course, that I undertook for myself a number of duties which are not usually part of a butler's life. I think my staff plan was as good as possible under the circumstances. However, I now realize that I gave myself too much to do.

You may be amazed that I failed to notice such an obvious weakness in the staff plan. But an accidental, external circumstance often brings to one's attention a simple truth. In this case, the circumstance was the arrival of Miss Kenton's letter.

The letter, with its happy memories of Darlington Hall, made me realize that I was making errors because I was overworked. And I was overworked because we were understaffed. I recalled Miss Kenton's great affection for this house, and her high professional standards. She was, I knew, just the person I needed to enable

3

me to complete a fully satisfactory staff plan for Darlington Hall.

As a result of this analysis of the situation, I was soon reconsidering Mr Farraday's kind suggestion. If I took his advice and had a few days' break, I would be able to drive to the West Country and visit Miss Kenton. I could then explore in more detail her wish to return to employment here at Darlington Hall.

I did not, however, discuss the matter with Mr Farraday for several days. I needed more time to consider the practicalities of the expedition: the cost, the time, the possibility that I might have misunderstood the purpose of Miss Kenton's letter. Mr Farraday himself might not have been serious in his offer. Eventually, I decided to speak to Mr Farraday about this as I served afternoon tea in the drawing room.

Mr Farraday has usually just returned from a short walk in the grounds at this time, and he is rarely busy. In fact, when I bring him afternoon tea, he often closes the book or journal that he is reading, stands up and stretches his arms in front of the windows. He appears to expect conversation with me.

I had forgotten, however, that, in the afternoon, Mr Farraday prefers humorous chat to serious conversation. He likes to banter. I should not, therefore, have mentioned the fact that a former housekeeper of Darlington Hall was living in the area that I was planning to visit. It gave Mr Farraday the opportunity to banter. He grinned at me and said:

'You surprise me, Stevens. A lady-friend. And at your age.'

Lord Darlington would never have placed an employee in such an embarrassing situation. But I do not mean to imply that Mr Farraday is unkind. He was, I am sure, simply enjoying the sort of bantering which, in the United States, may be a sign of a good, friendly understanding between employer and employee.

Bantering has been a regular feature of our relationship over the last few months, although I am still rather unsure of how to respond. When Mr Farraday first moved into Darlington Hall, I was once or twice astonished by some of the things he said to me. For example, I once asked him if a certain gentleman was likely to be accompanied by his wife on his visit to the house.

'God help us if she does come,' Mr Farraday replied. 'Maybe you could take her out, Stevens. You could take her to one of those stables around Mr Morgan's farm. She may be just your type.'

For a moment or two I had no idea what my employer was saying. Then I realized that he was making a joke and I attempted to smile appropriately. Over the following days I learnt not to be shocked by my employer's joking remarks. I smiled in the correct manner whenever I noticed a bantering tone in his voice. Nevertheless, I could never be sure what he expected of me on these occasions. Should I laugh, or should I respond with a similar type of remark? This last possibility has made me quite anxious. It is possible that my employer considers my inability to respond to his bantering as a serious failure of mine. I did once attempt to banter, but my employer simply looked up at me and said:

'I beg your pardon, Stevens?'

This was so discouraging that, I must admit, I have not made any more recent attempts. But, at the same time, I cannot help feeling that Mr Farraday is not satisfied with my various responses to his banter. You will understand, therefore, how uncomfortable the situation was for me yesterday afternoon. If I had replied to my employer's banter at that moment, the situation would only have become more embarrassing. I therefore said nothing.

'I didn't think you were a lady's man, Stevens,' Mr Farraday went on. 'Keeps the spirit young, I guess. But then I really don't know if I should help you with such improper activities.'

I smiled slightly, and continued to stand there awkwardly, waiting for my employer to give me permission to undertake the motoring trip. After a short delay, Mr Farraday kindly gave his permission and remembered his generous offer to pay for the petrol.

5

So now there seems little reason why I should not undertake my motoring trip to the West Country. I would, of course, have to write to Miss Kenton to tell her I might be in her area. I would also need to consider the matter of suitable clothes for the journey. There would be other questions concerning arrangements here in the house during my absence. But, on the whole, I can see no real reason why I should not go.

Chapter 2   Unfamiliar Territory

September 1956

Tonight, I have taken a room at a guest house in the city of Salisbury. The first day of my trip is completed and I feel quite satisfied with it.

It is hard to explain my feelings when I finally left Darlington Hall this morning. For the first twenty minutes of motoring, I cannot say that I was filled with excitement or anticipation. As I motored in the sunshine, I continued to be surprised by the familiarity of the countryside around me.

But eventually the surroundings became unrecognizable and I knew that I had gone beyond all previous boundaries. I confess, I experienced a mild sensation of alarm. This increased when I found myself on a road curving around the edge of a hill. I could sense the steep drop to my left, although I could not see it through the trees and thick bushes that lined the roadside. I felt now that I had truly left Darlington Hall behind, and I was suddenly afraid that I was not on the correct road. It was only the feeling of a moment, but it caused me to slow down. Even when I had assured myself that I was on the right road, I felt I had to stop the car for a moment to consider my situation.

I decided to get out and stretch my legs a little. When I had stepped out of the car, the feeling of being halfway up a steep hill increased. On one side of the road, the bushes and trees rose steeply. On the other, as I looked down through the trees, I could see the distant countryside. I suddenly decided that I wanted a clearer view, and I walked along the road until I found a narrow footpath which led up the hill.

I hesitated for a moment, for the path looked steep and rather rough. Then I began to climb. It was a long, hard walk, but it did not cause me any great difficulty. Finally, I came out of the trees and saw a bench in the middle of a small, open area. I walked to the bench and, turning round, I was pleased to see that the climb had not been a waste of time.

I had a most marvellous view of the surrounding countryside. There were hundreds of fields bordered by hedges and trees, and the land rose and fell gently towards the distant horizon. As I listened to the sounds of summer and felt the light wind on my face, my feelings of alarm and anxiety about leaving my familiar territory disappeared. I told myself that it was foolish to worry about meeting Miss Kenton again. Indeed, as I looked at that wonderful view, I even began to feel, for the first time, a sense of excitement at the journey ahead.

Now, this evening, I find myself in this small but comfortable guest house not far from the centre of Salisbury. The landlady, a woman of about forty, noticed my car and my high-quality suit, and seems to think that I am a rather grand visitor. When I wrote my address in her register as 'Darlington Hall', she looked at me with alarm. She probably assumed that I was a gentleman who was accustomed to expensive hotels, and that I would angrily leave her guest house as soon as I saw my room. But my room is very clean, with good-sized windows overlooking the street. It is perfectly adequate for my needs.

And here, in the quiet of this room, my thoughts return to that marvellous view this morning of the English countryside. I am willing to believe that other countries offer more dramatic scenery, although I have never had the privilege of observing those sights myself. But I am confident that the finest English countryside possesses a quality that the landscapes of other nations do not possess, the quality of 'greatness'.

But what exactly is this 'greatness'? Wiser heads than mine are needed to answer such a question, but I believe that the beauty of our land lies in its calmness, in its *lack* of obvious drama. The land, it seems, knows its own beauty, its own greatness, and feels no need to shout about it.

This reminds me of a question that has caused much debate in my profession over the years: what is a 'great' butler? There have been very few attempts to answer this question officially, but great butlers do seem to me to share one essential quality, and that is best described by the word dignity.

Of course, one can enjoy most interesting debates on the subject of what this 'dignity' actually is. To me, though, it is the butler's ability not to abandon his professional self under any circumstances. A great butler wears his professionalism as a decent gentleman wears his suit; he will take it off when, and only when, he chooses to. And this will always be when he is entirely alone.

It is sometimes said that butlers only truly exist in England; other countries have manservants. I believe this may be true. Continentals are unable to be butlers because they are incapable of the emotional self-control – the dignity – which only the English possess. For this reason, when you think of a great butler he must, almost by definition, be an Englishman.

Some of my colleagues have argued that attempts to analyse greatness are pointless; one can recognize immediately whether a person does or does not have it. But it is surely our professional responsibility to think deeply about these things. In this way we may make every effort to achieve 'dignity' for ourselves.

♦

I have rarely been happy in strange beds. It took me a long time to fall asleep last night, and I woke up over an hour ago while it was still dark. I tried to return to sleep but this was impossible. I decided therefore to get up.

Now, in these quiet moments as I wait for the world to awake, I am thinking about Miss Kenton's letter. I should perhaps explain that her name is not 'Miss Kenton' now. She has been 'Mrs Benn' for the last twenty years. However, I am unable to think of her as 'Mrs Benn', as I have not seen her since she married and moved to the West Country. I must continue to call her 'Miss Kenton', for this is how I have always thought of her.

Unfortunately, her letter has given me another reason for continuing to think of her as 'Miss Kenton'. It seems that her marriage has sadly come to an end. The letter does not contain details of the matter, and I would not expect it to. But Miss Kenton clearly says that she has now moved out of Mr Benn's house in Helston and is staying in the neighbouring village of Little Compton.

It is, of course, tragic that her marriage has ended in failure. Miss Kenton is now a lonely, unhappy, middle-aged woman and probably greatly regrets her decision to leave Darlington Hall. It is easy to see why she would want to return there now. It is true that she does not say this directly in her letter, but she speaks about the old days at Darlington Hall with such affection and nostalgia that I am sure that this is her real message.

Of course, Miss Kenton must realize that times have changed at Darlington Hall since she left twenty years ago. It will be my first duty to emphasize this when we meet. I will have to explain that the days of working with a large staff will almost certainly never return within our lifetime. But Miss Kenton is an intelligent woman. She probably already understands these things.

Miss Kenton's letter reveals at times a sense of hopelessness at her present situation, which worries me. She begins one sentence: *Although I have no idea how I shall usefully fill what remains of my life . . .* And again, elsewhere, she writes: *The rest of my life stretches out emptily before me.* The tone of most of the letter, however, is nostalgic. For example, she writes: *This whole incident reminds me of Alice White. Do you remember her? Who could forget her awful vowel sounds and ungrammatical sentences! Have you any idea what happened to her?*

I have no idea what happened to Alice White, although it amused me to remember her. After a very bad start, she became one of Darlington Hall's most devoted housemaids.

In another part of her letter, Miss Kenton writes: *I was so fond of that view from the second-floor bedrooms. I remember the lawn and the hills visible in the distance. Is it still like that? On summer evenings there was a magical quality to that view. I will confess to you now that I used to spend a lot of time in those bedrooms looking out of the windows.*

Then she adds: *If this is a painful memory, forgive me. But I will never forget standing with you at one of those bedroom windows. We were both watching your father. He was walking backwards and forwards in front of the summerhouse, looking at the ground. He seemed to be looking for a precious jewel that he had dropped there – do you remember?*

It surprises me that Miss Kenton can still remember this incident. It must have occurred on a summer evening over thirty years ago. I can clearly remember climbing to the second-floor landing. Evening sunlight shone through the half-open bedroom doors into the dark corridor. As I made my way along the corridor, I saw Miss Kenton standing by a window in one of the bedrooms. She turned as I was passing and called softly:

'Mr Stevens, do you have a moment?'

As I entered, Miss Kenton turned back to the window. Down below, the shadows of the trees were falling across the lawn. To the right, the lawn sloped up towards the summerhouse. And there was my father, walking slowly backwards and forwards, looking anxiously at the ground.

Chapter 3   Small Errors

1922

Miss Kenton and my father arrived at Darlington Hall at the same time. This was because the previous housekeeper and under-butler had decided to marry one another and leave the profession. My father had, until this time, been butler to Mr John Silvers at Loughborough House. When his employer died, my father lost his job and his accommodation. Although he was still, of course, a professional of the highest class, he was now in his seventies and was showing signs of his age. He would have found it difficult to find a new job in competition with younger butlers. It therefore seemed reasonable to ask my father to bring his great experience to Darlington Hall.

One morning, a short time after my father and Miss Kenton had joined the staff, I was working at the table in my office. Suddenly I heard a knock at my door. I was a little surprised when Miss Kenton opened the door and entered before I had given her permission. She came in holding a large vase of flowers and said with a smile:

'Mr Stevens, I thought these would brighten your room a little.'

'I beg your pardon, Miss Kenton?'

'Your room is so dark and cold, Mr Stevens, and there's such bright sunshine outside. I thought these would add a touch of colour.'

'That's very kind of you, Miss Kenton.'

She put her vase down on the table in front of me, then glanced around my office again. 'If you wish, Mr Stevens, I could bring in some more flowers for you,' she said.

'Miss Kenton, I appreciate your kindness,' I replied. 'But this is not a room of entertainment. More flowers will not be necessary.'

'But surely, Mr Stevens, there's no need to keep your room so dark and colourless.'

'I prefer my office to be like this, Miss Kenton, though I appreciate your thoughts. In fact, since you are here, there was something I wished to discuss with you.'

'Oh, really, Mr Stevens?'

'Yes, Miss Kenton, just a small matter. I was walking past the kitchen yesterday when I heard you calling to someone named William.'

'Did you, Mr Stevens?'

'Indeed, Miss Kenton. I heard you call several times for "William". May I ask whom you were talking to?'

'I was talking to your father, Mr Stevens. There are no other Williams in the house.'

'It is an easy error to make,' I said with a small smile. 'May I ask you, Miss Kenton, to refer to my father as "Mr Stevens" in future? I would be very grateful.'

I returned to my work but, to my surprise, Miss Kenton did not leave. 'Excuse me, Mr Stevens,' she said after a moment.

'Yes, Miss Kenton.'

'I'm afraid I don't quite understand. I'm accustomed to using the servants' first names. It is usual, I believe.'

'A most understandable error, Miss Kenton. However, you must understand that you are speaking to my father, not just another servant.'

'I still don't understand, Mr Stevens. I believe I am the housekeeper of this house, while your father is the under-butler.'

'He is of course the under-butler, as you say. But I am

surprised that you have not noticed that he is, in fact, much more than that.'

'I have obviously been very unobservant, Mr Stevens. I have only noticed that your father is an excellent under-butler.'

'Then you have not observed him carefully enough, Miss Kenton. If you had, you would have realized that it is not appropriate for someone of your youth and inexperience to call my father by his first name.'

'Mr Stevens, I may not have much experience, but I am considered by many to be good at my job.'

'I am sure you are an excellent housekeeper, Miss Kenton. But you should have realized that my father is a man of great experience. You would learn many things from him if you observed him more carefully.'

'I am grateful to you for your advice, Mr Stevens. So do please tell me, what marvellous things might I learn from observing your father?'

'That is obvious to anyone with eyes, Miss Kenton.'

'But I thought we had already agreed, Mr Stevens, that my powers of observation are not as good as they should be.'

'Miss Kenton, if you believe that you are already a perfect housekeeper, you will never reach the top of your profession. I have noticed, for example, that you are still often unsure of where to put certain items.'

Miss Kenton said nothing for a moment. Indeed, she looked a little upset. Then she said:

'I had a little difficulty when I first arrived, but that is surely only normal.'

'Exactly, Miss Kenton. If you had observed my father, who arrived in this house a week after you did, you would have seen that he made no mistakes at all. His house knowledge was perfect from the beginning.'

Miss Kenton seemed to think about this before saying:

13

'I am sure Mr Stevens senior is very good at his job, but I assure you, Mr Stevens, I am very good at mine. I will remember not to use your father's first name in future. Now, please excuse me.'

After this meeting, Miss Kenton made no more immediate attempts to bring flowers into my office. I also noticed that she stopped using my father's first name. However, one afternoon two weeks later, she came into the library where I was working and said:

'Excuse me, Mr Stevens. But if you are searching for your dustpan, it is out in the hall.'

'I beg your pardon, Miss Kenton?'

'Your dustpan, Mr Stevens. You have left it out here. Shall I bring it in for you?'

'Miss Kenton, I have not been using a dustpan.'

'Ah, well, then forgive me, Mr Stevens. I naturally assumed you were using your dustpan and had left it out in the hall. I am sorry to have disturbed you.'

She started to leave, but then turned at the doorway and said:

'Oh, Mr Stevens. I would return it myself but I am busy at the moment. I wonder if you will remember it?'

I waited until Miss Kenton had gone upstairs, then I crossed the library and looked out into the hall. There, in the middle of the polished floor, was a dustpan.

This was an unimportant, but annoying error. The dustpan could have been seen not only from the five ground-floor doorways, but also from the stairs and the first-floor landings. Then, as I moved across the hall to pick it up, I suddenly realized the importance of this mistake.

My father had been brushing the entrance hall half an hour earlier. At first, I found it hard to believe that my father could have made such an error. But I soon reminded myself that everybody makes mistakes from time to time. I began, instead, to feel annoyed with Miss Kenton for exaggerating the importance of such a small mistake.

A week later, as I was coming down the back corridor from the kitchen, Miss Kenton came out of her room. She wanted to tell me that there were remains of polish on the dining-room silver.

'The end of one of the forks is almost black,' she informed me.

I thanked her for this information, and she returned to her room. She did not need to say, of course, that my father was responsible for polishing the silver.

There were probably other similar incidents, which I have now forgotten, but things soon reached a climax. One grey, wet afternoon, while I was polishing Lord Darlington's sporting cups in the games room, Miss Kenton entered and said from the door:

'Mr Stevens, I have just noticed something outside which puzzles me.'

'What is that, Miss Kenton?'

'The Chinaman which normally stands on the landing is now outside this door.'

'I'm afraid, Miss Kenton, that you are a little confused.'

'I don't believe I am confused at all, Mr Stevens. If you don't believe me, perhaps you will come and see for yourself?'

'I am busy at present, Miss Kenton.'

'But Mr Stevens, you must come and see for yourself if you don't believe me.'

'I will look at it later, Miss Kenton. There is no hurry.'

'Does that mean that you believe me, Mr Stevens?'

'I don't know, Miss Kenton. I must see for myself.'

'Then come and see.'

'I have already told you, Miss Kenton, I am busy.'

I returned to my business, but Miss Kenton remained in the doorway, observing me. Eventually, she said:

'I can see you don't have much more to do, Mr Stevens. I'll wait outside for you.'

With those words, she left the room.

I spent as long as I could polishing Lord Darlington's cups in the games room, thinking that Miss Kenton would soon become bored with waiting for me. Eventually, however, there were no more tasks for me to do and I had to leave. To my surprise, when I walked out into the corridor, I saw that Miss Kenton was still waiting for me. I turned and walked away from her as quickly as I could, but she ran and stood in front of me. I was forced to stop.

'Mr Stevens,' she said. 'That is the incorrect Chinaman, do you not agree?'

'Miss Kenton, I am very busy. I am surprised you have nothing better to do than stand in corridors all day.'

'Mr Stevens, is that the correct Chinaman or is it not?'

'Miss Kenton, I must ask you to keep your voice down.'

'And I must ask you, Mr Stevens, to turn around and look at that Chinaman.'

'Miss Kenton, please! What would the other employees think if they heard us shouting at the top of our voices about Chinamen?'

'The fact is, Mr Stevens, all the Chinamen in this house have been dirty for some time! And now they are in incorrect positions!'

'Miss Kenton, you are being ridiculous. Kindly let me pass.'

'Mr Stevens, will you kindly look at the Chinaman behind you?'

'If it is so important to you, Miss Kenton, I admit that it is possible that the Chinaman has been placed incorrectly. But I really cannot understand why you are so worried about such unimportant errors.'

'These errors may be unimportant, Mr Stevens, but you must realize their larger significance.'

'Miss Kenton, I do not understand you. Would you kindly let me pass?'

'The fact is, Mr Stevens,' she said, 'your father has too much responsibility for a man of his age. He is too old to cope with it. He is making more and more mistakes. If you don't take notice of them now, something much more serious is going to happen.'

'Miss Kenton, you are making yourself look foolish.'

'I'm sorry, Mr Stevens, but I must go on. I believe there are many jobs your father should not be expected to do at his age. He should not have to carry heavy trays. Have you seen the way his hands tremble? One day soon, a heavy tray will fall from his hands on to a lady's or gentleman's lap. And furthermore, Mr Stevens – and I am very sorry to say this – I have noticed your father's nose.'

'Have you indeed, Miss Kenton?'

'Yes, I have, Mr Stevens. The evening before last I watched your father walking very slowly towards the dining room with his tray. I regret to say that I clearly saw a large drop on the end of his nose hanging over the soup bowls. If a lady or gentleman had seen that, Mr Stevens, I am sure they would have lost their appetite.'

Chapter 4   An Embarrassing Fall

The more I think about it, the less certain I am that Miss Kenton spoke to me on that day as boldly as I have just reported. It was still early in our relationship, and I am sure that she did not say things like:

'These errors may be unimportant, but you must realize their larger significance.' In fact, I think it was Lord Darlington who used those words.

March 1923

Two months after my conversation with Miss Kenton about the Chinaman, Lord Darlington called me into his study. The situation concerning my father had become very serious because it was after he had had his accident.

Whenever Lord Darlington wished to speak to me about something, he often pretended to be reading a book. He would wait for me to pass, then he would look up from his book and say:

'Oh, Stevens. There was something I meant to say to you.'

I am describing this small detail in order to show that Lord Darlington was a shy and modest man. A lot of nonsense has been spoken and written recently about his lordship.* Many reports have criticized the part he played in this country before and during the war. They claim that he was a selfish and foolish man. Let me say here that all these reports about him are completely false. Lord Darlington was a good man with a good heart. I am proud to have given my best years of service to such a true gentleman.

On this particular afternoon, Lord Darlington hardly looked up from his book as he asked:

'Your father feeling better now, Stevens?'

'Much better now, thank you, sir.'

'Very pleased to hear that. Very pleased.'

There was a short, uncomfortable pause, then Lord Darlington said:

'I wonder, Stevens, have there been any – well – *signs* at all? Any indications that your father might prefer an easier life these days? Work a little less hard, I mean?'

'I believe, sir, that you can still completely depend on him to do his job. It is true that he has made one or two errors recently, but none of them has been serious.'

'That's true, Stevens. But nevertheless, we don't want to see an accident like that again, do we? It could happen during dinner, while he was serving at table.'

* *his lordship*: a respectful way of referring to a lord.

18

'It is possible, sir.'

'Listen, Stevens. The first guests will be arriving here for the conference in less than a fortnight. What happens within this house may be very important for our country. I am not exaggerating, Stevens. We cannot possibly afford to have any accidents then.'

'Indeed not, sir.'

'I am not suggesting that your father should leave us, Stevens. I am simply asking you to reconsider his duties.' His lordship then looked down again into his book and said: 'These errors may be unimportant, Stevens, but you must realize their larger significance. Another accident might threaten the success of our conference in two weeks' time.'

'Indeed, sir. I fully understand.'

Lord Darlington had witnessed my father's accident himself a week or so earlier. He had been with two guests, a young lady and gentleman, in the summerhouse and had seen my father crossing the lawn with a tray of refreshments. As my father began to climb the stone steps to the summerhouse, however, he fell. By the time I reached the scene of the accident, his lordship and his guests had turned my father on to his side and had tried to make him comfortable. My father was unconscious, and his face was strangely grey in colour. With the help of a wheelchair, my father was transported with difficulty into the house. By the time Doctor Meredith arrived, my father had woken up and was beginning to feel better.

The whole incident was clearly a great embarrassment to my father, but he soon forgot about it and returned to work. It was not easy, therefore, for me to tell him that it had been decided to reduce his work load. He was a proud man. Another difficulty for me was the fact that my father and I hardly ever talked to each other. For several years, even the smallest professional conversation had seemed to embarrass us. I had never really understood why.

In the end I decided to talk to my father privately in his room.

19

Early one morning, I climbed up to the top floor of the house and knocked gently on his door. My father was sitting on the edge of his bed in full uniform. He had obviously been sitting there for some time.

'Ah,' I said, and gave a short laugh. 'I thought Father would be up and ready for the day.'

'I've been up and ready for the last three hours,' he said, looking me up and down rather coldly.

'I have come here to tell you something, Father.'

'Then be quick. I haven't all morning to listen to you.'

'The fact is, Father has been making a number of errors recently. His lordship believes – and I agree with him – that he is working too hard for a man of his age. His lordship is very worried about the smooth running of this house. He does not want any more unfortunate accidents, especially during next week's important international conference.'

My father's face, in the half-light, showed no emotion.

'It has been decided, therefore, that Father should no longer have to serve at table.'

'I have served at table every day for the last fifty-four years,' my father said slowly and calmly.

'Furthermore,' I continued, 'it has been decided that Father should not carry trays. I have here a list of his new duties.'

I did not wish, for some reason, to hand him the piece of paper directly, so I placed it on the end of his bed. My father glanced at it, then looked at me again. Eventually he said:

'I only fell that time because of the steps. They're not straight.'

'Indeed. Now, I hope that Father will study this sheet of new duties. Good morning.'

That summer evening which Miss Kenton mentioned in her letter came very soon after that conversation. Indeed, it may have been the evening of that same day. As I have said before, I can remember the evening sunlight shining through the open

20

bedroom doors into the dark corridor. And as I was walking past the bedrooms, Miss Kenton called to me.

I stood next to her by the window and looked down. We could see my father standing by the stone steps in front of the summerhouse. A soft wind blew through his hair and there was a deep frown on his face. Then, as we watched, he walked very slowly up the steps. At the top he turned and came back down, a little faster. He repeated this several times, his eyes never once leaving the ground. It was exactly as Miss Kenton describes it in her letter: *He seemed to be looking for a precious jewel that he had dropped there.*

♦

Some people might consider me to have been rather insensitive when I spoke to my father about his declining abilities. But the fact is, I had to deal with the problem in an impersonal and businesslike manner – as I am sure you will agree when I have explained the situation in more detail.

Lord Darlington had been preparing for the conference of March 1923 for many years. He had made his first trip to Berlin in 1920, and was unhappy when he returned to Darlington Hall. When I asked him how he had enjoyed his trip, he said:

'Upsetting, Stevens. Deeply upsetting. It is not right for us to treat a defeated enemy like this. The war ended two years ago. We are making the people of Germany suffer too much. It is not like the British to be so unforgiving.'

After that, Lord Darlington spent more and more time trying to help the German people. Powerful and famous gentlemen became regular visitors to the house. Many of them came in secret, so I am unable to reveal their names to you. Some of the guests were so secret that I was not permitted to tell the staff who they were. However – and I say this with pride – his lordship never hid things from me.

Over the following two years, his lordship and a close friend of his, Sir David Cardinal, became the leaders of a powerful and important group of people who all agreed that the people of Germany had suffered enough. They believed that if the economic crisis in Germany became any worse, all of Europe would be in danger.

By the beginning of 1922, his lordship had a clear plan. He wanted an 'unofficial' international conference at Darlington Hall. He would invite people from European governments who agreed with his ideas about helping Germany. After this conference, these people would return to their countries and attempt to change their governments' attitudes towards Germany.

As the date for the conference approached, the pressures on me began to increase. It was my responsibility to make sure that nothing went wrong. If any of the guests were, for some reason, dissatisfied with their stay at Darlington Hall, it could threaten the success of the conference. Great damage might be done to the future peace of Europe.

However, it was not possible for me to plan things as carefully as I wanted. I was aware that there would be twenty guests – eighteen gentlemen and two ladies. Each guest, however, was going to arrive with a team of secretaries and servants, and nobody knew exactly how many. It was impossible for me, therefore, to know how many rooms would be needed. Furthermore, a number of guests would be arriving some time before the conference, but nobody knew the exact dates of these arrivals.

I prepared for the conference like a general preparing for a battle. I produced a staff plan, and held a special meeting with everybody who worked in the house.

'I know you all have a lot of extra work to do,' I told them. 'We are all under great pressure, but you can take great pride in performing your duties in the days ahead. It is possible that history will be made under this roof!'

The staff knew that I was not the kind of person to make

exaggerated statements. They understood that something extraordinary was going to take place.

This was the general atmosphere of Darlington Hall at the time of my father's accident. It was only two weeks before the conference, and I had many other urgent problems to think about. You will understand, therefore, why I might have seemed a little insensitive with my father when I informed him of the reduction in his duties.

Chapter 5   The Birds and Bees

In the busy days just before the conference, there was a great change in my father's behaviour. He had a trolley loaded with cleaning equipment, teapots, cups and saucers. He seemed filled with a strange, youthful energy, and he pushed his trolley all around the house. He moved so quickly that a stranger might have thought that there were several men pushing trolleys around Darlington Hall, not just one.

The increasing pressure of the days just before the conference affected Miss Kenton, too, although in a completely different way.

I remember, for example, meeting her in the back corridor. I reminded her that the sheets for the bedrooms on the upper floor needed to be ready.

'The matter is perfectly under control, Mr Stevens,' she replied.

I began to move away, but Miss Kenton took one more step towards me with an angry expression on her face.

'Unfortunately, Mr Stevens, I am extremely busy now,' she said. 'I wish I had as much spare time as you do. Then perhaps I too could happily wander about this house and remind *you* of tasks that you have perfectly under control.'

'Now, Miss Kenton, there is no need to be so bad-tempered. I simply wanted to remind you . . .'

'This is the fourth or fifth time this week, Mr Stevens, that you have reminded me to do something that I have already done,' she interrupted me. 'It is very strange to see you with so much spare time that you have nothing better to do.'

'Miss Kenton, you must be very inexperienced if you think that I have any spare time. I hope that, in future years, you will understand more clearly how difficult it is to organize a great house like this.'

'You are always talking about my "great inexperience", Mr Stevens, but have you noticed anything wrong with my work? If you had, I'm sure you would have told me about it before now. Now, I have a lot of work to do. I would be grateful if you would stop interrupting me like this. If you have so much spare time, I suggest that you go for a walk outside and get some fresh air.'

With those words, she marched past me along the corridor. I was so surprised that I did not know what to do at first. Then, deciding that it was best not to say anything, I continued on my way. I had, however, almost reached the kitchen doorway when I heard the sound of angry footsteps coming back towards me again.

'In fact, Mr Stevens,' she called, 'I would be grateful if, in future, you did not speak to me directly at all. If it is necessary to communicate with me, please use a messenger. Or you may like to write a note and have it sent to me. Now, I must return to my work. And you can continue to wander around the house criticizing people for no reason!'

Although I was annoyed by Miss Kenton's behaviour, I had no time to think about it because the first guests had arrived. Two Foreign Office* officials and Lord Darlington's friend, Sir David Cardinal, had arrived before the other guests to discuss the conference. As I went in and out of the various rooms in which these four gentlemen sat, I could not avoid hearing parts of their

* Foreign Office: the government department responsible for international affairs.

24

conversation. They seemed to be talking most of the time about one man – an extremely important Frenchman whom I shall call Monsieur Dupont. On one occasion, I came into the smoking room and heard one of the gentlemen saying:

'The future of Europe depends on persuading Dupont that we are right.'

In the middle of these discussions, his lordship asked me to perform a rather unusual task. He called me into his study, sat down at his desk and, as usual, pretended to start reading a book.

'Oh, Stevens,' he began. Then he did not seem to know how to continue, for he turned a page of his book and fell silent. A few moments later he tried again. 'Stevens, I realize that this is a strange request.'

'Sir?'

'It's just that I have so much to think about at present.'

'I would be very glad to assist, sir.'

'I'm sorry to have to ask you to do a thing like this, Stevens. I know you must be extremely busy yourself. But I can't think of any other solution.'

He studied the book in front of him for several long seconds before continuing, without looking up:

'You are familiar, I assume, with the facts of life.'

'Sir?'

'The facts of life, Stevens. Birds, bees, that sort of thing.'

'I'm afraid I don't quite understand, sir.'

'Let me be frank, Stevens. Sir David is a very old friend of mine. He's brought his son, Reginald, to our conference as his secretary. Young Reginald is engaged to be married.'

'Yes, sir.'

'Sir David has been trying to tell his son the facts of life for the last five years. The young man is now twenty-three.'

'Indeed, sir.'

'Well, Stevens, this is the problem. Sir David has asked me, as his oldest friend, to tell young Reginald about the facts of life. Sir David himself is nervous about doing it. He thinks it would be much better if *I* performed the task. The trouble is, I'm so busy with this conference . . .'

His lordship paused and went on studying the page.

'Do I understand, sir, that you wish *me* to give young Mr Cardinal the necessary information?'

'If you don't mind, Stevens. It would be a great help. Sir David continues to ask me every couple of hours if I've done it yet.'

'I see, sir. It must be very difficult for you.'

'Of course, I realize what an awkward task this is, Stevens.'

'I will do my best, sir,' I assured his lordship. 'It might, however, be difficult for me to find the right moment to deliver the information.'

'I'd be grateful if you even tried, Stevens. It's very decent of you. But listen, there's no need to go into great detail. Just give him the basic facts, that's all.'

An hour after my conversation with Lord Darlington, I noticed young Mr Cardinal alone in the library. He was sitting at one of the writing tables, working on some documents. Deciding to perform my awkward task as quickly as possible, I entered the library and gave a little cough.

'Excuse me, sir, but I have a message for you,' I said.

'Oh, really?' said Mr Cardinal, looking up from his papers. 'From Father?'

'Yes, sir. In an indirect sort of way.'

The young gentleman reached down into the black bag at his feet, brought out a notebook and pencil and said:

'I'm ready, Stevens.'

I coughed again and said:

'Sir David wishes you to know, sir, that ladies and gentlemen are different in a number of ways.'

I must have paused a little to consider the wording of my next sentence, because Mr Cardinal said:

'I am aware of that, Stevens.'

'You are aware, sir?'

'My father constantly underestimates me, Stevens. I've done quite a lot of reading on the subject.'

'Really, sir. Then, in that case, perhaps my message is unnecessary.'

'You can assure Father that I have discovered everything I need to know. This bag is full of notes I have made on the subject.'

'Indeed, sir?'

'Unless, of course, Father has new information he wants me to think about. Is there anything more, for example, on this Dupont fellow?'

'I believe not, sir,' I said, attempting to hide my disappointment. I thought I had successfully completed the task, but found instead that I hadn't even started it. However, before I could make another attempt on the subject, Mr Cardinal rose to his feet and said:

'Well, I think I'll go outside for some fresh air, Stevens. Thanks for your help.'

I had intended to speak again to Mr Cardinal immediately, but that afternoon – two days earlier than expected – Mr Lewis, the American senator, arrived. More guests arrived the next morning: two ladies from Germany who had brought with them a large team of servants as well as a great many trunks. Then, in the afternoon, an Italian gentleman arrived. He was accompanied by a servant, a secretary, an adviser and two security men.

Several more guests arrived the following day, and Darlington Hall was already filled with people of all nationalities two days before the conference began. Although the guests were always polite to each other, there was a strange atmosphere in the house. The visiting servants seemed to look at one another very coldly, and my own staff were glad to be too busy to spend much time with them.

One afternoon, while I was becoming increasingly busy with

the many demands made of me, I glanced out of a window and saw young Mr Cardinal. He was taking some fresh air around the grounds. Although I had much more important things on my mind, I immediately thought of the task which Lord Darlington had asked me to perform, and which I had not yet completed. I decided that this was a suitable time and place for me to deliver the message.

I crossed the grass quickly and waited behind a bush until I heard Mr Cardinal's footsteps along the path that bordered the lawn. Unfortunately, I misjudged the timing of my appearance from behind the bush. I had intended to come out on to the path while Mr Cardinal was still some distance away. I could have pretended to notice him for the first time, and started a conversation with him in a natural manner. However, I moved out from behind the bush a little too late, and, I regret to say, I frightened the young gentleman. He stepped backwards in alarm, holding his black bag tightly.

'I'm very sorry, sir.'

'Stevens. You gave me a shock.'

'I'm very sorry, sir,' I repeated. 'But I have a message to deliver to you. If I may speak directly, sir. You will notice the geese not far from us.'

'Geese?' He looked around, a little confused.

'And also the flowers and bushes. This is not, in fact, the best time of year to see them, but you will appreciate, sir, that in spring we will see a change – a very special sort of change – in these surroundings.'

'Yes, I'm sure this is not the best time of year to see the grounds. But frankly, Stevens, I wasn't paying much attention to the beauty of nature. It's all rather worrying. That Monsieur Dupont has arrived in a very bad mood.'

'Monsieur Dupont has arrived here at this house, sir?'

'About half an hour ago. He's in a terrible temper.'

'Excuse me, sir. I must attend to the matter immediately.'

'Of course, Stevens. It was kind of you to come out here and talk to me.'

'Please excuse me, sir, but I have not quite finished my message on the topic of – as you say – the beauty of nature. If you would allow me to continue on another occasion, I would be most grateful.'

'I shall look forward to it, Stevens. Although I'm more interested in fish than flowers and geese. I know all about fish.'

'All living creatures will be relevant to our future discussion, sir. However, you must now please excuse me. I had no idea that Monsieur Dupont had arrived.'

With those words I hurried back to the house.

Monsieur Dupont was a tall, elegant gentleman with a grey beard. He had arrived in the sort of clothes that European gentlemen often wear on their holidays. As Mr Cardinal had said, Monsieur Dupont had not arrived in a good temper. A lot of things had upset him since his arrival in England. Among other things, he had painful sores on his feet after sightseeing in London. I told his manservant to speak to Miss Kenton, but this did not prevent Monsieur Dupont from shouting at me every few hours:

'Butler! I need some more bandages!'

His mood seemed to improve, however, when he saw Mr Lewis. He and the American senator greeted each other as old colleagues. They went everywhere together, chatting quietly or laughing about old memories. The other guests, meanwhile, did not go near Monsieur Dupont. They seemed suspicious of him, which somehow seemed to emphasize his importance to the conference.

Chapter 6   The Conference

The conference began on a rainy morning during the last week of March. On the first morning, I had to go constantly in and out of the drawing room, where all the serious, dark-jacketed gentlemen had gathered. I noticed that Monsieur Dupont did not speak very much. Once, while I was leaving the room in the middle of a speech by a German gentleman, Monsieur Dupont rose to his feet and followed me out.

'Butler,' he said, as soon as we were in the hall. 'I wonder if I could have the bandages on my feet changed. They are so uncomfortable that I can hardly listen to these gentlemen.'

I sent a messenger to ask Miss Kenton for assistance, then left Monsieur Dupont sitting in the games room. However, just as I was going to continue my duties, the first footman came down the stairs towards me. He informed me that my father had suddenly become very ill upstairs.

I hurried up to the first floor and, when I reached the landing, I saw something very strange. My father was at the far end of the corridor. He was kneeling on the floor with both hands on the trolley. He had bowed his head and seemed to be staring at something on the carpet. He did not move at all. Two housemaids were standing beside him, not knowing what to do. I went to my father, released his hands from their grip on the trolley and gently lowered him on to the floor. His eyes were closed, and his face was covered in sweat. I called for more help, and my father was eventually put in a wheelchair and taken up to his room.

When my father was in bed, I did not know what to do. I did not want to leave him but, on the other hand, I was too busy to stay. As I hesitated in the doorway, Miss Kenton appeared at my side and said:

'Mr Stevens, I'm not as busy as you are. If you like, I can look after your father. I'll bring Doctor Meredith up and tell you if he has anything important to say.'

'Thank you, Miss Kenton,' I said, and I went downstairs.

I returned to the drawing room and was immediately busy serving the guests tea and coffee. A short time later, as I was leaving the drawing room with an empty teapot in my hand, Miss Kenton stopped me and said:

'Mr Stevens, Doctor Meredith is leaving now.'

The doctor was putting on his hat and coat in the hall when I arrived. The teapot was still in my hand.

'Your father's not good,' he said. 'If he gets worse, call me again immediately.'

I thanked the doctor and showed him out.

♦

The next day, the discussions in the drawing room were much more serious. Several of the guests seemed to be getting angry with Monsieur Dupont and were making bold accusations against him. The French gentleman did not reply. He just sat quietly in his armchair and stroked his beard. Whenever there was a break in the conference, Mr Lewis took Monsieur Dupont away to a quiet corner and whispered to him in private.

Meanwhile, my father's condition remained the same. When I had a spare moment, which was not often, I went up to his room and found him asleep. I did not, therefore, have a chance to talk to him until the second evening.

On that occasion, too, he was sleeping when I entered the room. But the housemaid stood up when she saw me and began to shake my father's shoulder.

'Foolish girl!' I said. 'What do you think you are doing?'

'Mr Stevens asked me to wake him if you returned, sir,' she replied, and shook my father's shoulder again.

My father opened his eyes, turned his head a little and looked at me.

'I hope Father is feeling better now,' I said.

He stared at me for a moment, then asked:

'Everything under control downstairs?'

'It is very busy in the kitchen at the moment, as Father can imagine.'

An impatient look crossed my father's face. 'But is everything under control?' he said again.

'Yes, I can assure Father that it is. I'm glad that Father is feeling better.'

Very slowly, he took his arms from under the bedclothes and stared tiredly at the backs of his hands. He continued to do this for some time.

'I'm glad Father is feeling so much better,' I repeated. 'Now really, I should get back. As I say, it is very busy in the kitchen at the moment.'

He went on looking at his hands for a moment. Then he said slowly:

'I hope I've been a good father to you.'

I laughed a little and said:

'I'm so glad you're feeling better now.'

'I'm proud of you. You're a good son. I hope I've been a good father to you. I suppose I haven't.'

'I'm afraid we're extremely busy now, but we can talk again in the morning.'

My father continued to look at his hands. He seemed to be slightly annoyed with them.

'I'm so glad you're feeling better now,' I said again, and left the room.

♦

At the second and final dinner of the conference, the guests seemed friendlier and more relaxed than they had throughout the previous days. I and my staff served much more wine than we had before. At the end of the dinner Lord Darlington rose to make a speech.

He thanked his guests for coming to the conference, and proceeded to talk for a long time about his hopes for a better future for Europe. When he had finally sat down, everybody was surprised to see Monsieur Dupont rise to his feet. There was immediate silence in the room. He thanked Lord Darlington for his hard work, and everybody in the room voiced quiet approval. He then surprised everybody by criticizing the American senator, Mr Lewis, for trying to create trouble between him and the other guests at the conference. When he eventually sat down, there was an awkward silence. Finally Mr Lewis rose to his feet and proceeded to criticize Lord Darlington for not understanding the problems of the real world – for not being a professional, like him. 'The world is too complicated for true gentlemen to understand,' he said. 'It's time for politicians and businessmen to take control.'

When he had finished speaking, there was a shocked silence and no one moved. Then Lord Darlington stood up and defended himself against Mr Lewis's attacks. He talked about honour, justice and goodness. 'Professionalism,' he said, 'is just another word for greedy dishonesty.'

Everybody in the room clapped with great enthusiasm at this part of his lordship's speech, except for Mr Lewis. He just looked into his wine glass and shook his head with a tired smile. Just at that moment, I became aware of the first footman beside me.

'Miss Kenton would like a word with you, sir,' he whispered. 'She's just outside the door.'

I left as quietly as possible while his lordship was still speaking. Miss Kenton looked rather upset.

'Your father has become very ill, Mr Stevens,' she said. 'I've called for Doctor Meredith, but I believe he may be a little late.'

I must have looked a little confused, for Miss Kenton then said:

'Mr Stevens, he really is in a bad state. You had better come and see him.'

'I only have a moment. The gentlemen will be needing me in the smoking room very soon.'

'Of course. But you must come now, Mr Stevens, otherwise you may deeply regret it later.'

When I arrived in my father's room, Mrs Mortimer, the cook, was standing by his bed. My father's face had gone a dull, reddish colour. I had never seen that colour in a living person's face before. I looked at my father for a moment, touched his forehead slightly, then withdrew my hand.

'In my opinion,' Mrs Mortimer said, 'he's suffered a stroke.' With that she began to cry. I turned away and said to Miss Kenton:

'This is most upsetting. Nevertheless, I must now return downstairs.'

'Of course, Mr Stevens. I will tell you when the doctor arrives.'

I hurried downstairs and was in time to see the gentlemen going into the smoking room. There was now a genuine atmosphere of celebration among the guests as I moved around the crowded smoking room with my tray. I had just finished serving a glass to a gentleman when a voice behind me said:

'Ah, Stevens, you're interested in fish, you say.'

I turned to find the young Mr Cardinal smiling happily at me. I smiled also and said:

'Fish, sir?'

'When I was young, I used to keep tropical fish in a tank . . . My God, Stevens, are you all right?'

I smiled again. 'Quite all right, thank you, sir.'

'As you so rightly explained, I really should come back here in spring. Darlington Hall must be lovely then. The last time I was here . . .' Mr Cardinal stopped again and looked at me. 'Are you *sure* you're all right, Stevens?'

'Perfectly all right, thank you, sir.'

'Not feeling unwell, are you?'

'Not at all, sir. Please excuse me.'

I proceeded to serve drink to some other guests. Then I felt something touch my elbow and turned to find Lord Darlington.

'Stevens, are you all right?'

'Yes, sir. Perfectly.'

'You seem to be crying.'

I laughed and, taking out a handkerchief, I quickly wiped my face. 'I'm sorry, sir. The strains of a hard day.'

'Yes, it's been hard work.'

I was continuing around the room when I saw Miss Kenton standing in the doorway. She signalled for me to go over to her. I began to make my way towards the doors but, before I could reach them, Monsieur Dupont touched my arm.

'Butler,' he said, 'I wonder if you would find me some fresh bandages. My feet are hurting again.'

'Yes, sir.'

As I moved towards the doors, I realized Monsieur Dupont was following me. I turned and said:

'I will come and find you, sir, as soon as I have the bandages.'

'Please hurry, butler. I am in pain.'

'Yes, sir. I'm very sorry, sir.'

As I entered the hall, Miss Kenton walked silently towards the stairs. Then she turned and said:

'Mr Stevens, I'm very sorry. Your father died about four minutes ago.'

'I see.'

She looked at her hands, then up at my face. 'Mr Stevens, I'm very sorry,' she said. Then she added:

'I wish there was something I could say.'

'There is no need, Miss Kenton.'

'Doctor Meredith has not arrived yet.' For a moment she bowed her head. She seemed to be crying. But almost immediately she looked up again and said in a steady voice:

'Will you come up and see him?'

'I'm very busy now, Miss Kenton. Soon, perhaps.'

'Then, Mr Stevens, will you permit me to close his eyes?'

'I would be most grateful, Miss Kenton.' She began to climb the stairs, but I stopped her and said: 'Miss Kenton, please don't think that I'm cold-hearted because I'm not coming up to see my father at this moment. You see, I know my father would have wished me to continue working just now.'

'Of course, Mr Stevens.'

I turned away and re-entered the smoking room. As I was moving among the guests with my tray, Monsieur Dupont touched my shoulder and said:

'Butler, have you found my bandages yet?'

'I'm very sorry, sir.'

'What's the problem, butler? Why haven't you found them yet?'

'Sir, a doctor is on his way.'

'Ah, very good! You called a doctor.' Monsieur Dupont turned away and continued his conversation. A short time later, a footman approached me and said:

'Miss Kenton would like to have a word with you, sir.'

I made my way towards the doors, but noticed that Monsieur Dupont was guarding them.

'Butler, is the doctor here?' he asked.

'I am just going to find out, sir. I won't be a moment.'

'I am in pain.'

'I'm very sorry, sir. The doctor should not be long now.'

This time, Monsieur Dupont followed me out of the door. Miss Kenton was again standing in the hall.

'Mr Stevens,' she said. 'Doctor Meredith has arrived and gone upstairs.'

36

She had spoken in a low voice, but Monsieur Dupont behind me immediately said:

'Ah, good!'

I turned to him and said:

'Perhaps you would follow me, sir.'

I led Monsieur Dupont into the games room, then returned to the hallway. Miss Kenton was still waiting for me. Without a word, she accompanied me up the stairs to my father's room.

Doctor Meredith, who was sitting by my father's bed, stood up when I arrived and said:

'I'm sorry, Stevens. He suffered a severe stroke. I can assure you, however, that he was not in any pain.'

'Thank you, sir.'

'I'll be on my way, now. You'll make the arrangements?'

'Yes, sir. However, would you mind seeing a gentleman downstairs? He is in need of your attention.'

'Urgent?'

'He is very keen to see you, sir.'

I led Doctor Meredith downstairs, showed him into the games room, then returned to the smoking room, where the atmosphere among the guests had grown even more cheerful than before.

Chapter 7   Silver

September 1956

I am now on the third day of my trip to the West Country. Last night I stayed in an inn named *The Coach and Horses,* an attractive, quiet-looking cottage just outside the market town of Taunton in Somerset. Unfortunately, however, the inn was not as quiet as it had seemed when I arrived. Although the landlord's wife did not actually shout, I could hear her talking late into the night and, again, early this morning. As a consequence, I slept rather badly, although I did not, of course, say anything about this when I thanked the landlord and his wife this morning.

Now, however, I am enjoying a pleasant mid-morning cup of tea in a small tearoom in the high street of Taunton, very close to the market square. Although I am sitting at the back, I can see clearly out into the sunlit street. There is an interesting signpost on the pavement opposite the tearoom. It is pointing to several local destinations, one of which is the village of Mursden.

Giffen and Company once had a factory in the Somerset village of Mursden This company was famous for manufacturing polish. Giffen's polish was the finest silver polish available for many years. Then, just before the war, new chemical substances became available and the demand for Giffen's silver polish began to decline.

Giffen's silver polish first appeared at the beginning of the 1920s. In my opinion, it was responsible for an important change of attitude in my profession. The polishing of silver suddenly became a central part of a butler's responsibilities. Before Giffen's existed, the butlers of my father's age did not consider the polishing of silver so important. But in the 1920s, the full significance of silver was recognized by the younger butlers. Visitors to a house would examine the silver during a meal more closely than anything else. Guests would often judge the quality of a house by its silver.

I, of course, was very aware of the appearance of this new, high-quality product, and I immediately made the polishing of silver my top priority. I can remember with pride many occasions when visitors to Darlington Hall commented on the silver. Lady Astor once said our silver shone more brightly than any silver she had seen. Mr George Bernard Shaw, the famous writer, came to dinner one evening and held a silver dessert spoon up to the light. But perhaps my proudest moment was when Lord Halifax, the government minister who later became head of the Foreign Office, came to dinner.

This visit was the first of a series of 'unofficial' meetings arranged by Lord Darlington between Lord Halifax and the German Ambassador, Herr Ribbentrop. Lord Halifax, on that first night, had been very suspicious when he arrived at Darlington Hall. He was not happy about meeting the German Ambassador in secret like this. Lord Darlington suggested a tour of Darlington Hall. In the past, this had often helped many nervous visitors to relax. However, Lord Halifax continued to express his doubts about the evening as he walked around the rooms. Lord Darlington tried to reassure him, but without success. But then, as I was going about my business, I heard Lord Halifax say:

'My God, Darlington, the silver in this house is a delight.'

I was, of course, very pleased to hear this at the time. Two or three days later I was even more satisfied when Lord Darlington told me:

'By the way, Stevens, Lord Halifax was very impressed with the silver the other night. It put him in a very good mood.'

I honestly believe, therefore, that the high quality of the silver that evening was probably responsible for the success of Lord Halifax's first meeting with Herr Ribbentrop.

I should, perhaps, now say a few words concerning Herr Ribbentrop. Nowadays, of course, most people believe that Herr Ribbentrop was just a liar. They say that he was part of Hitler's plan to deceive the English for as long as possible – to stop the English from understanding his true intentions. I do not wish to disagree with this view. It is, however, rather annoying when people today say that they always knew Herr Ribbentrop was a liar. They say that Lord Darlington was the only man in England who believed that the German Ambassador was an honest gentleman.

The truth is very different. In the mid-1930s, Herr Ribbentrop was a welcome guest in the very best houses. The same people who invited Herr Ribbentrop to their homes say now that Lord Darlington betrayed his country. In my opinion, anyone who suggests that his lordship was secretly trying to help the enemy is conveniently forgetting the true atmosphere of those times.

I would also like to correct another false accusation, which is now often made against Lord Darlington. It is nonsense to claim, as people do, that his lordship disliked Jews. People who make these claims know nothing about the sort of gentleman Lord Darlington was. I heard him express his disgust on several occasions when somebody made insulting comments about Jews. And the accusation that his lordship never allowed Jewish people to enter the house or any Jewish staff to be employed is completely false. Except, perhaps, for one minor incident in the 1930s . . .

But I am moving away from the subject of silver. Perhaps I should not spend so much time looking back to the past. After all, I still have before me many more years of service. Mr Farraday is not only a most excellent employer. He is an American gentleman, and one has a special duty to show him all that is best about service in England. It is essential, then, to keep one's mind on the present, and not on the achievements of the past. It is, unfortunately, true that, over these last few months, things have not been perfect at Darlington Hall. There have been a number of small errors, including one incident last April concerning the silver. Fortunately, Mr Farraday had no guests, but it was nevertheless a moment of genuine embarrassment to me.

It occurred at breakfast one morning. After sitting at the table, Mr Farraday picked up a fork, examined it for a brief second, then turned his attention to the newspaper. While he was reading, I moved quickly to remove the fork from the table. I took it immediately to the kitchen and returned without delay with another fork. I thought for a second about putting the fork quietly on to the tablecloth without attracting Mr Farraday's attention. But then I thought it was possible that Mr Farraday did not want to embarrass me, and was only pretending not to have noticed. I therefore decided to put the new fork down on the table with a certain emphasis. This made my employer look up from his newspaper and say:

'Ah, Stevens.'

Errors like this have been, as I have already said, a result of the shortage of staff. If Miss Kenton returned to Darlington Hall, these errors would, I am sure, no longer be made. Of course, I must not forget that Miss Kenton says nothing directly in her letter about wishing to return.

Last night, when I was unable to sleep because of the noise in the small inn outside Taunton, I read her letter again carefully. It was surprisingly difficult to identify any passage which clearly indicated her desire to return.

But, on the other hand, it seems foolish to worry about such things. Within forty-eight hours I will be face to face with Miss Kenton. I shall be able to discover for myself whether she truly wishes to return to Darlington Hall or not.

Chapter 8   Sarah and Ruth

I should perhaps, at this point, return to the question of Lord Darlington's attitude towards Jewish people. I want, in particular, to discuss the false belief that Lord Darlington banned Jews from working on the staff at Darlington Hall. I am in the perfect position, as head of staff, to deny these accusations absolutely. There were many Jewish people on the staff throughout all my years with his lordship, and they were never treated differently as a result of their race. The only possible reason for these ridiculous accusations is, perhaps, one brief incident in the summer of 1932.

41

One afternoon, his lordship called me into his study.

'I've been doing a lot of thinking, Stevens,' he said. 'And I've decided that we cannot have Jews on the staff here at Darlington Hall.'

'Sir?'

'It is for the good of this house, Stevens. In the interests of the guests we have staying here.'

'Of course, sir.'

'Tell me, Stevens, we have a few Jews on the staff at the moment, don't we?'

'I believe two of the present staff come into that category, sir.'

'Ah.' His lordship paused for a moment, staring out of his window. 'Of course, you'll have to dismiss them. It's regrettable, Stevens, but we have no choice. I've thought about this very carefully. It's in all our best interests.'

The two Jewish members of staff were both housemaids. It was right, therefore, to speak to Miss Kenton first and inform her of the situation. I decided to do this that same evening when I met her for cocoa in her room.

I should perhaps say a few words here about these meetings in her room at the end of the day. Our conversations were completely professional, although some informal topics were discussed from time to time. Our reason for having these meetings was simple: our lives were so busy that we hardly had time to speak to each other during the day. This lack of communication was a serious danger to the continued smooth running of operations in Darlington Hall. Fifteen minutes in private together at the end of the day in Miss Kenton's room seemed, therefore, the simplest solution to the problem.

I was a little anxious about telling Miss Kenton that I had to dismiss two of her maids. They had both been perfectly satisfactory employees, and I was not personally in favour of dismissing them. Nevertheless, it would have been irresponsible of me to display my true feelings on the matter. It was a difficult task, but it had to be performed with dignity.

When I finally introduced the subject towards the end of our conversation that evening, I was as clear and as businesslike as possible. I finished by saying:

'I will speak to the two maids in my office tomorrow morning at ten thirty. I would be grateful, Miss Kenton, if you could send them to me.'

At first, Miss Kenton said nothing. So I continued:

'Well, Miss Kenton, thank you for the cocoa. It is time for me to go to bed. Another busy day tomorrow.'

As I was leaving, Miss Kenton suddenly said:

'Mr Stevens, I cannot quite believe my ears. Ruth and Sarah have been members of my staff for over six years. They have served this house excellently.'

'I'm sure that is true, Miss Kenton. However, we must not allow personal feeling to affect our judgement.'

'Mr Stevens, I'm shocked that you can sit there and speak about this so calmly. You are saying that Ruth and Sarah have to be dismissed because they are Jewish?'

'Miss Kenton, I have just explained the situation to you. His lordship has made his decision and there is nothing for you or I to debate.'

'Have you not considered, Mr Stevens, that it would be quite *wrong* to dismiss Ruth and Sarah because they're Jewish? I will not work in a house in which such things can occur.'

'Miss Kenton, please do not excite yourself. Remember your position. This is a very simple matter. If his lordship wishes to end their contracts, there is no more to be said.'

'I'm warning you, Mr Stevens, I will not continue to work in such a house. If my girls are dismissed, I will leave too.'

'Miss Kenton, may I suggest that you and I are not in a position to judge what is right and what is not. The world of today is a very complicated and dangerous place. His lordship is in a much better position than we are to judge what is best. Now, Miss Kenton, I really must go to bed. I thank you again for the cocoa. Send the two employees to me at ten thirty tomorrow morning, please.'

As soon as the two maids stepped into my office the following morning, I could see that Miss Kenton had already spoken to them. They both came in crying. I explained the situation to them as briefly as possible, emphasizing the fact that their work had been satisfactory. The whole interview lasted perhaps for three or four minutes, and they were still in tears when they left.

Miss Kenton was extremely cold towards me for some time afterwards. At times she was quite rude to me, even in front of the staff. Although we continued our habit of meeting for cocoa in the evening, our conversation was brief and her tone unfriendly. When there had been no improvement in her behaviour after a fortnight, I started to become a little impatient. I therefore said to her one evening:

'Miss Kenton, I am surprised that you haven't left yet.' I accompanied this with a little laugh to show that I was joking. Miss Kenton, however, was not amused. She frowned at me and said:

'I still intend to leave, Mr Stevens. I have been too busy to organize it, that's all.'

This made me think that she was, perhaps, serious about her threat. But then, as the weeks passed, it became clear that she was not going to leave Darlington Hall. The atmosphere between us gradually improved, and I began to joke about her threat to resign. For example, if we were discussing a future large occasion to be held at the house, I sometimes finished the conversation by saying:

'Of course, Miss Kenton, if you are still with us.'

Even months after the event, such remarks still made Miss Kenton go quiet – although I think that this was due more to embarrassment than anger.

Eventually, of course, we stopped mentioning the subject. But I remember one last reference to it more than a year after the maids had left.

His lordship mentioned it one afternoon when I was serving his tea in the drawing room.

'Oh, Stevens,' he said to me. 'I've been meaning to talk to you about that business last year. About the Jewish maids. Do you remember?'

'Indeed, sir.'

'I suppose there's no way of finding out where they are now, is there? It was wrong, what happened. One would like to compensate them for it somehow.'

'I will certainly investigate, sir. But I am not sure that it will be easy to discover their whereabouts after all this time.'

'See what you can do, Stevens. That business should never have happened.'

I thought that Miss Kenton would be interested in what his lordship had said, and I decided to mention it to her – even at the risk of getting her angry again. However, when I finally spoke to her about it, my conversation with her produced strange results.

One foggy afternoon, I was crossing the lawn towards the summerhouse in order to clear away some cups and saucers. As I approached the steps where my father had once fallen, I noticed a figure moving about inside the summerhouse. It was Miss Kenton. When I entered, however, she had stopped moving about and was sitting down on a chair, apparently busy with some needlework. When I looked more closely, I noticed that she was repairing a cushion.

As I began to gather up the cups and saucers, Miss Kenton and I talked to each other about unimportant things. It was a pleasant change to be outside in the summerhouse after so many continuous days in the main building. Neither of us was in a hurry to return indoors. As the daylight rapidly faded and the fog began to thicken over the lawn, Miss Kenton and I often stopped working and stared out of the windows in silence. Then, during one of our silences, I finally introduced the topic of the maids' dismissal.

'I was just thinking earlier, Miss Kenton,' I said. 'It is rather funny to remember now, but only a year ago you were still insisting you were going to resign. It rather amused me to think of it.' I gave a laugh, but behind me Miss Kenton remained silent. When I finally turned to look at her, she was staring quietly through the windows at the fog.

'You probably have no idea, Mr Stevens,' she said eventually, 'how seriously I thought of leaving this house. I felt so strongly about what happened.' She paused for a while, and I turned my attention back to the window. Then she continued in a tired, dreamy voice:

'I was a coward, Mr Stevens. I did not leave because I had nowhere to go. I have no family, only my aunt. I love her dearly, but I can't live with her for a day without feeling that my life is wasting away. I told myself, of course, that I would soon find another job somewhere. But I was so frightened, Mr Stevens. I feel so ashamed of myself.'

Miss Kenton paused again and seemed to be deep in thought. I thought that this was an appropriate moment for me to inform her of my recent conversation with Lord Darlington. I finished by saying:

'The past cannot be undone. But it is, at least, comforting to hear his lordship say that it was all a terrible mistake. I just thought you would like to know, Miss Kenton, since I recall that you were as upset by the incident as I was.'

'I'm sorry, Mr Stevens,' Miss Kenton said behind me in an entirely new voice. 'I don't understand you.'

I turned in surprise and saw that Miss Kenton was no longer looking dreamily out of the window. She was staring directly at me with a look of challenge in her eyes.

'As I recall, Mr Stevens, you thought that it was right and proper for Ruth and Sarah to leave. You were positively cheerful about it.'

'Now really, Miss Kenton, that is quite incorrect and unfair. The whole matter upset me terribly. It is hardly the sort of thing I like to see happen in this house.'

'Then why, Mr Stevens, did you not tell me this at the time?'

I gave a laugh, but for a moment was rather lost for an answer. Before I could think of one, Miss Kenton put down her sewing and said:

'Do you realize, Mr Stevens, how much it would have meant to me if you had shared your feelings with me last year? You knew how upset I was when my girls were dismissed. Why, Mr Stevens, why, why, why do you always have to *pretend*?'

I gave another laugh. The conversation was, in my opinion, becoming rather ridiculous. 'Really, Miss Kenton,' I said. 'I'm not sure I know what you mean.'

'I suffered so much over Ruth and Sarah leaving us. And I suffered more because I believed I was alone.'

'Really, Miss Kenton . . .' I picked up the tray of cups and saucers. 'Naturally, I disapproved of the dismissals. I thought that was obvious.'

She did not say anything and, as I was leaving, I glanced back towards her. She was again looking out at the view, but it had by now grown very dark inside the summerhouse. I could only see the dark shape of her figure against a pale and empty background. I excused myself and walked out into the fog.

Chapter 9   Lisa

One of the replacements for the two dismissed maids was a young woman called Lisa. I remember not being very impressed with her references. Moreover, when Miss Kenton and I interviewed her, it became clear that she had never remained in the same job for longer than a few weeks. Her whole attitude suggested to me that she was quite unsuitable for employment at Darlington Hall. To my surprise, however, Miss Kenton was extremely keen to employ her.

'This girl has a bright future,' she insisted, despite my protests. 'I will be responsible for her, Mr Stevens. I will make sure that she does well.'

I continued my protests, but Miss Kenton eventually won the argument. To my amazement, her judgement on the matter seemed to be correct. During the following weeks, the young girl made extremely good progress. Her attitude and her manner of walking – which, during the first days, had been so bad that I had to look away – improved dramatically.

As the weeks passed, Miss Kenton took great delight in her victory. She enjoyed giving Lisa tasks that required more and more responsibility. If I was watching, she would smile at me with a victorious look in her eyes.

'No doubt, Mr Stevens,' she said to me one night as we drank our cocoa, 'you will be extremely disappointed to hear Lisa has still not made any serious mistakes.'

'I'm not disappointed at all, Miss Kenton. I will admit, you have had some modest success with the girl.'

'Modest success! Look at that smile on your face, Mr Stevens. It always appears when I mention Lisa. That smile tells an interesting story. A very interesting story indeed.'

'Really, Miss Kenton? And may I ask, what story is that?'

'It is very interesting that you have been so critical of her from the beginning, because Lisa is a pretty girl. And I've noticed that you dislike having pretty girls on the staff.'

'You know perfectly well you are talking nonsense, Miss Kenton.'

'Ah, but I've noticed it, Mr Stevens. Is it possible that our Mr Stevens feels uncomfortable with pretty girls? Perhaps our Mr Stevens is flesh and blood after all and cannot completely trust himself?'

'Really, Miss Kenton, you're making no sense. I shall simply sit and think of other things while you go on talking.'

'Ah, but why then is that guilty smile still on your face, Mr Stevens?'

'It is not a guilty smile at all, Miss Kenton. I am slightly amused by your ability to talk nonsense, that's all.'

'It *is* a guilty smile, Mr Stevens. And I've noticed how you can hardly bear to look at Lisa. Now it is becoming very clear why you didn't want her on the staff.'

'The girl was completely unsuitable when she first came to us, as you well know.'

Our conversation continued in this way for several more minutes. Of course, we would never have talked in this way in front of the other staff. But our cocoa evenings, although still basically professional in tone, had begun to allow room for a little harmless talk of this nature. Playful conversations like this helped us to relax after the demands of a busy working day.

However, eight or nine months after she had joined us, Lisa disappeared from the house with a footman. This kind of thing is, unfortunately, a normal part of life for any butler of a large house. It is extremely annoying when it happens, but one learns to accept it.

They had also both left letters. The footman, whose name I cannot remember, left a short note addressed to me. It said something like, *Please do not think too badly of us. We are in love and are going to get married*. Lisa had written a much longer note addressed to 'the Housekeeper'. Miss Kenton brought this note into my office the morning after their disappearance. The letter, which was full of spelling and grammar mistakes, talked about how much in love the couple were, and their plans for a future life together. One line said: *We don't have money but who cares we have love and who wants anything else we've got one another.* Although the letter was three pages long, Lisa did not once thank Miss Kenton for the kindness she had shown her.

Miss Kenton was clearly upset. As I was reading the young woman's letter, she sat at the table before me, looking at her hands. When I had put the letter down on the table, she said:

'So, Mr Stevens. It seems you were right and I was wrong.'

'Miss Kenton, there is no reason for you to blame yourself. These things happen.'

'I was wrong, Mr Stevens. I accept it.'

'Miss Kenton, I cannot agree with you. You achieved great things with that girl. You must not blame yourself for anything.'

Miss Kenton continued to look unhappy. She said very quietly:

'You're very kind, Mr Stevens. I'm very grateful.' Then she said, in a tired voice:

'She's so foolish. She might have had a real career ahead of her. She had ability. So many young women like her throw away their chances, and for what?'

We both looked at the notepaper on the table between us, then Miss Kenton turned her head away with annoyance.

'Indeed,' I said. 'Such a waste, as you say.'

'So foolish. And the girl is sure to be disappointed. She could have become a housekeeper one day, but she's thrown it all away. All for nothing.'

'It really is most foolish of her,' I agreed.

I started to gather up the sheets of paper in front of me, planning to keep them in my office, but then I hesitated. I was not sure whether Miss Kenton had intended me to keep the letter or not. I therefore put the pages back down on the table between us and looked at Miss Kenton. But she seemed far away, lost in thought.

'She's sure to be disappointed,' she said again. 'So foolish.'

Chapter 10   A Lonely Hill

September 1956

I have, it seems, become rather lost in these old memories. This was never my intention. But thinking about the past has at least helped me to forget the events of this evening. For, I have to admit, these last few hours have been extremely difficult for me.

I am now staying in an upstairs room of a small cottage in the tiny village of Moscombe in Devon. It belongs to a retired couple called Mr and Mrs Taylor. It is very kind of the Taylors to allow me to stay in this room. Mrs Taylor has not only made the bed for me, she has tidied and cleaned the room, too. Although I have repeatedly offered to pay for the room, they have refused to accept a penny.

I am staying in this cottage because I made one foolish, annoyingly simple, mistake. I had forgotten to check the petrol. It is true, I had been thinking about other things just before the car stopped. I had planned to stay in the town of Tavistock, but I could not find a room anywhere because of an agricultural fair. After I had tried several inns and guest houses, one landlady suggested that I should drive to a roadside inn which belonged to a relative of hers.

She gave me thorough directions, which had seemed clear enough at the time, but I was unable to find this roadside inn. Instead, after about fifteen minutes, I was driving along a misty road that curved across wild, open land. To my left, I could see the last red light of the sunset. Through the mist, I could see the distant shape of an occasional farm building. Apart from these, there was no sign of civilization.

I turned the Ford round and drove back, trying to find a road I had passed earlier. After some time I managed to find it, but I was still lost. This new road was even more isolated than the one I had just left. I drove in near-darkness between high hedges, then the road began to climb steeply. By now, I had given up hope of finding the roadside inn. I decided to drive on until I reached the next town or village. Halfway up the hill, however, the engine made a strange noise, and I noticed for the first time that the petrol tank was empty.

The Ford continued to climb for several more metres, then stopped. When I got out of the car, it was almost completely dark. I was standing on a steep road bordered by trees and hedges. Further up the hill I could see, through a break in the hedges, the shape of a wooden gate against the sky. I made my way up towards this gate, hoping to find a farmhouse or something. I was disappointed to find, however, that instead of a farmhouse there was just open land.

I stopped at the gate and stared across the fields. The land sloped downwards about twenty metres from the gate and disappeared into shadow. About two kilometres further ahead, the land rose into sight again, and I could see the distant shape of a church. Around the church there were small clouds of white smoke rising from chimneys.

I admit that I felt, at that moment, a little discouraged, but I tried to be positive. The situation was not absolutely desperate, I told myself. The Ford was not damaged, simply out of fuel. It would take me about half an hour to walk across the fields to the village. When I was there, I was sure to find accommodation and a can of petrol from somewhere. Nevertheless, despite these positive thoughts, I did not feel happy up there on that lonely hill, looking over the gate through the mist and darkness at the lights of a distant village.

After returning to the Ford to collect my case and a bicycle lamp, I searched for a footpath that might take me to the village. I was, however, unable to find one, so I had to climb over the gate and walk across the fields. The journey was not as bad as I had imagined. It consisted of a series of fields, each one muddier than the last. The worst thing was when I tore the shoulder of my jacket while squeezing through a small gap in one of the hedges.

Eventually I discovered a path which led down into the village. On my way along this path I met Mr Taylor. He touched his cap when he saw me with my torn clothes, muddy shoes, bicycle lamp and case. He then asked if I needed any help. When I explained my situation to him, Mr Taylor shook his head thoughtfully and said:

'I'm afraid there's no inn in our village, sir. But if you don't mind something less comfortable, my wife and I could offer you a room and a bed for the night. It's nothing special. It used to be our son's room before he went to live in Exeter.'

I protested that I did not wish to cause him and his wife so much inconvenience, but he paid no attention and said:

'It would be an honour to have you, sir. We don't get gentlemen like you passing through Moscombe very often. Besides, sir, I don't know what else you could do at this hour.'

Chapter 11   Secrets

When I said earlier that this evening's events had been extremely difficult, I was not only referring to the fact that I had had to walk for half an hour in complete darkness across muddy fields. In many ways, what occurred during supper with Mr and Mrs Taylor and their neighbours was even worse than that. After supper, it was a great relief for me to come up to this room and to be alone with my thoughts and my memories.

I have recently been spending more and more time thinking about the old days at Darlington Hall. Since I received the letter from Miss Kenton, I have tried to understand what happened to our relationship. We had developed a fine professional understanding over many years. Then, in 1935 or 1936, things started to go wrong between us. By the end of this period, we had even abandoned our routine cup of cocoa together at the end of the day. But, despite all the time I have spent thinking about this, I have never been able to decide the exact moment when things between us began to change.

1935–36

One important turning point in our relationship might have been the evening when Miss Kenton came uninvited into my office. I cannot remember now why she came. However, I do clearly remember her words:

'Mr Stevens, your room looks even worse at night than it does in the day. That electric bulb isn't bright enough. You'll ruin your eyes trying to read by that light.'

'It is perfectly comfortable, thank you, Miss Kenton.'

'Really, Mr Stevens. This room looks like a prison cell.'

I did not reply to this. I continued with my reading, waiting for Miss Kenton to excuse herself and leave. But a few minutes later I was surprised to hear her voice again:

'I wonder what you are reading there, Mr Stevens.'

'Simply a book, Miss Kenton.'

'But what sort of book?'

I looked up and saw Miss Kenton walking towards me. I shut the book and rose to my feet.

'Really, Miss Kenton,' I said, holding the book close to me, 'this is my own private time. I must ask you not to disturb me like this.'

'But why are you so shy about your book, Mr Stevens? Is it something embarrassing? A naughty book, perhaps?'

'There are no "naughty" books – as you call them – on his lordship's shelves.'

'Then you have no reason to be shy, Mr Stevens. So you can let me see what you are reading.'

'Miss Kenton, I must ask you to leave me alone. I do not have much free time for myself, and you are disturbing the little free time that I have.'

But Miss Kenton continued to advance. I was tempted for a moment to lock the book away in my desk, but this seemed over-dramatic. I took a few steps back.

'Please show me the book,' Miss Kenton insisted. 'Then I promise I will leave you alone to your reading.'

'The book is not important, Miss Kenton,' I replied. 'But I do object to this interruption of my private time.'

She continued to smile playfully. 'Perhaps, Mr Stevens, the book is so naughty that you want to protect me from its shocking influence?'

She was now standing in front of me, and my back was pressed against the wall. Then suddenly there was a peculiar change in the atmosphere. I am afraid it is not easy to describe what I mean by this. I can only say that everything around us suddenly became very still. Miss Kenton's playful smile disappeared and there was a sudden seriousness in her expression. She seemed to be almost frightened of something.

'Please, Mr Stevens. Let me see your book.'

She reached forward and began gently to release the book from my grip. I judged it best to look away while she did this. However, because her face was so close to mine, I had to twist my head away from her at a very unnatural angle. Miss Kenton continued to lift my fingers off the book – one at a time – until finally I heard her say:

'Mr Stevens, this book isn't naughty at all. It's simply a love story.'

At these words, I decided that I could stand no more. I cannot remember exactly what I said, but I remember showing Miss Kenton firmly out of the office.

Perhaps I should explain here something about the book I was reading. It is true, it was only a love story – one of many kept in the library and guest bedrooms for the entertainment of lady visitors. I agree that these love stories are usually very silly, and I rarely had the time or the desire to read any of them from cover to cover. But I had a simple reason for reading these books: it was an efficient way of developing my command of the English language.

In my opinion, it is extremely important for a butler to have a good accent and command of language, and I have always considered it my duty to develop them as much as I could. One way of doing this is to read a few pages of a well-written book whenever one has a spare moment. Love stories are, in my opinion, especially suitable for developing one's command of language. The characters speak in an elegant way, which is of great practical value to me. A more serious book may improve one's mind, but would not develop one's ability to hold normal conversations with ladies and gentlemen.

But I am moving away from the incident with Miss Kenton in my office. It brought to my attention something that I had not realized before: the fact that things between Miss Kenton and myself had gradually become, over a period of many months, too familiar. After I had shown Miss Kenton from my office, I decided that we had to return to a more professional relationship in future.

This was not, however, the only incident between Miss Kenton and myself that led to the great changes in our relationship. There were other equally important developments that might explain what took place later. For example, there was the matter of Miss Kenton's free days.

♦

Until about a month before the incident with my book, Miss Kenton's free days had followed a regular pattern. Every six weeks she would take two days off to visit her aunt in Southampton. Apart from this, she would follow my example of only taking days off if we were going through a quiet time.

But then the pattern changed. She suddenly began to use all her free time, and she disappeared regularly from the house without saying where she was going. Of course, she never took more time than she was allowed, so I felt it was not my business to ask her about her little trips. But I suppose this change in her routine did worry me a little, for I remember talking about it to Mr Graham. He was a regular visitor to our house because he was the butler to Sir James Chambers, an old friend of Lord Darlington's.

I had not intended to talk to Mr Graham about Miss Kenton. I had only mentioned that the housekeeper had been 'a little moody' recently. I was therefore rather surprised when Mr Graham nodded, leaned towards me and said:

'I'd been wondering how much longer it would be.'

When I asked him what he meant, Mr Graham explained:

'How old is Miss Kenton now? Thirty-three? Thirty-four? She has missed her best mothering years, but it's not too late yet.'

'Miss Kenton,' I assured him, 'is a devoted professional. I know that she has no wish for a family.'

But Mr Graham smiled and shook his head, saying:

'Never believe a housekeeper who tells you she doesn't want a family. You and I have known at least a dozen housekeepers who said they didn't want families, then got married and left the profession.'

I could not accept Mr Graham's theory at first. Afterwards, however, I must admit that I began to suspect that Miss Kenton had an admirer. There were little signs which seemed to support Mr Graham's theory. For instance, I noticed that Miss Kenton had started to receive letters about once a week. I also noticed sudden changes in her general mood which I had not noticed before. Sometimes she became extremely cheerful for no apparent reason. I do not know why, but this alarmed me more than the times when she suddenly became silent and depressed. She was always thoroughly professional, of course, and I had no reason to complain about her work. Nevertheless, it was my duty to think about the future of the house. I therefore asked her about her plans one evening while we were drinking our cocoa:

'Will you be going out again on Thursday, Miss Kenton? On your day off, I mean.'

Instead of being angry at my question, as I had expected, Miss Kenton actually seemed rather pleased to discuss this topic with me.

'Oh, Mr Stevens,' she said, 'it's just someone I once knew when I was at Granchester Lodge. In fact, he was the butler there at the time, but now he's left service altogether and he works for a local business. He somehow found out that I was here and started writing to me. In one of his letters a few weeks ago, he suggested that we meet occasionally in town.'

'I see, Miss Kenton. I'm sure it is a good idea to leave the house at times.'

Miss Kenton agreed, and there was a short silence. Then she went on:

'I remember when he was butler at Granchester Lodge, he had very ambitious ideas. I'm sure he planned, one day, to become butler of a house like this. Oh, but when I think of some of his methods! I'm not surprised that he never progressed in his career.'

I gave a small laugh. 'At these higher levels, Miss Kenton, the profession is not for everybody. Without certain qualities, a butler will simply not progress beyond a certain point.'

Miss Kenton seemed to consider this for a moment, then said:

'It occurs to me, Mr Stevens, that you are a contented man. You are at the top of your profession. I really cannot imagine what more you might wish for in life.'

I could think of no immediate response to this. There was an awkward silence, during which Miss Kenton stared down into her cocoa. In the end, after some consideration, I said:

'I will not be perfectly content, Miss Kenton, until I have done everything I can to help his lordship through the great tasks that he has set himself. Only when his lordship's work is complete, Miss Kenton, will I be able to call myself a contented man.'

She may have been a little puzzled by my words, or perhaps in some way they displeased her, for her mood suddenly seemed to change. Our conversation rapidly lost its personal tone and became more formal.

Not long after this, we stopped having meetings over cocoa in her room. In fact, I can remember our last cocoa together very clearly. I was discussing with her the complicated plans I had made for a weekend gathering of important people from Scotland. When I had been talking for a while, I realized that Miss Kenton was contributing very little to our conversation. It was obvious that she was thinking about something else. I did, from time to time, stop talking in order to ask her:

'Do you understand, Miss Kenton?' Then her attention would briefly return, before floating away again a few seconds later. After several more minutes of this, I finally said to her:

'I'm sorry, Miss Kenton, but I can see no reason to continue our conversation. You do not seem to appreciate the importance of this discussion.'

'I'm sorry, Mr Stevens,' she said, sitting up a little. 'It's just that I'm rather tired this evening.'

'You are increasingly tired now, Miss Kenton. You never used to make tiredness your excuse.'

To my amazement, Miss Kenton responded to this with sudden anger:

'Mr Stevens, I have had a very busy week. I am very, very tired, Mr Stevens. Can you not understand that?'

I decided not to enter into an argument with her. I paused for a moment before saying quite calmly:

'If that is how you feel about it, Miss Kenton, there is no need for us to continue with these evening meetings. I had no idea how inconvenient they had become to you.'

'Mr Stevens, I only said that I was tired tonight . . .'

'No, no, Miss Kenton, it is perfectly understandable. There are many other ways for us to communicate with each other without having to meet every evening.'

Miss Kenton made more protests, but she could not change my mind. There was no point in continuing our evening meetings if she was always too tired to say anything.

'May I suggest,' I said finally, 'that in future we communicate important information to each other during the working day. If we are unable to find each other, I suggest that we leave written messages. Now, Miss Kenton, I apologize for keeping you up so long. Thank you for the cocoa.'

Chapter 12   Miss Kenton's Aunt

Over the following weeks, Miss Kenton suggested several times that we start meeting again over cocoa in the evenings. I have often wondered whether things would have happened differently if I had agreed. It seems clear to me now that my small decision to stop our evening meetings was, in fact, another important turning point in our relationship.

But, I suppose, if one keeps searching one's past for 'turning points', one will start seeing them everywhere. Perhaps the most important 'turning point' of all was neither of the two incidents I have just described. Perhaps it was my meeting with Miss Kenton in the dining room soon after she had heard of her aunt's death.

News of the death had arrived some hours earlier. Indeed, I had handed the letter to Miss Kenton myself. I had stepped inside her room for a brief moment to discuss a professional matter, and she had opened the letter while we sat at her table, talking. She suddenly became very still, but she showed no emotion as she read the letter through at least twice. Then she put the letter carefully back in its envelope and looked across the table at me.

'It is from Mrs Johnson, a companion of my aunt. She says my aunt died the day before yesterday. The funeral takes place tomorrow. I would be grateful if I could have the day off, Mr Stevens.'

'I am sure that can be arranged, Miss Kenton.'

'Thank you, Mr Stevens. Forgive me, but perhaps I may have a few moments alone.'

'Of course, Miss Kenton.'

I made my exit but, just after I had left her room, I realized that I had not offered her my condolences. Her aunt had been like a mother to her, and her death must have come as a terrible shock. I paused outside her door in the corridor, wondering if I should go back and say a few words. But then it occurred to me that she might prefer to be alone with her private grief. I hesitated for several minutes outside her door. Eventually, however, I decided that it would be best to express my condolences later, and I continued on my way.

I thought about Miss Kenton all morning, wondering how I could help her in her time of grief, but I did not see her again until the afternoon. I was busy with a task in the hall when I heard her footsteps entering the dining room. I waited for a couple of minutes, then followed her in.

'Ah, Miss Kenton,' I said. 'How are you this afternoon?'

'Quite well, thank you, Mr Stevens.'

'Is everything in order?'

'Yes, thank you.'

'I was wondering about the new members of staff. Have you been experiencing any problems with them?' I gave a small laugh. 'There are often problems when so many new people join the staff at once.'

'Thank you, Mr Stevens, but the new girls are very satisfactory.'

'You don't think that there should be any changes to the present staff plan?'

'I don't think so, Mr Stevens. However, if I change my view on this, I will let you know immediately.'

She turned her attention back to her work and, for a moment, I thought about leaving the dining room. In fact, I actually took a few steps towards the doorway, but then I turned to her again and said:

'So, Miss Kenton. The new members of staff are making good progress, you say?'

'They are both doing very well, I assure you.'

'Ah, that is good to hear.' I gave another short laugh. 'I was only wondering because neither girl has previous experience of working in a house of this size.'

'Indeed, Mr Stevens.'

I watched her while she worked, waiting to see if she would say anything more. When, after several moments, it became clear that she was not going to speak, I said:

'There is actually something that I would like to say, Miss Kenton.'

Miss Kenton glanced over her shoulder in my direction, but continued working.

'I have noticed that there has been a slight fall in standards recently, Miss Kenton. One or two errors have been made. I do feel that you need to pay a little more attention to the new members of staff.'

'Whatever do you mean, Mr Stevens?'

'I myself like to pay extra attention to things whenever there are new staff members. I check everything, and see how they behave with other members of staff. I regret to say this, Miss Kenton, but I believe you have been a little careless in the matter.'

For a second, Miss Kenton looked confused. Then she turned towards me, and a certain strain was visible in her face.

'I beg your pardon, Mr Stevens?'

'For instance, Miss Kenton, I have noticed that the dishes are not being put back correctly on the shelves in the kitchen.'

'Indeed, Mr Stevens?'

'Yes, Miss Kenton. Furthermore, that little corner outside the breakfast room has not been dusted for some time. And there are one or two other small things I could mention.'

'You have made your point, Mr Stevens. I will, as you suggest, check the work of the new maids.'

'It is not like you to be so forgetful, Miss Kenton.'

Miss Kenton looked away from me with a look of confusion on her face. She looked more tired than upset. Then she suddenly turned away from her work, said, 'Please excuse me, Mr Stevens,' and left the room.

But it is pointless now to wish that particular incidents had ended differently. Naturally, when one looks back on moments like this, they may indeed seem to be 'turning points'. But of course, at that time, these things did not seem so important. There seemed to be a never-ending number of days, months and years ahead – plenty of time in which to sort out the small problems that existed between Miss Kenton and me. There was nothing at the time to indicate that small incidents like these would, in the end, be responsible for destroying whole dreams.

Chapter 13   A Difficult Evening

September 1956

I see that my memories are becoming more and more upsetting. This is probably because of the difficult evening I have just had. My present mood is also possibly connected to the fact that tomorrow – if I can find some petrol – I shall be arriving in Little Compton and I shall be seeing Miss Kenton again for the first time in twenty years.

Of course, I expect our interview to be polite and professional in character. The most important thing is for me to discover whether Miss Kenton is interested in returning to Darlington Hall or not. I have to confess that, having re-read her letter, I am beginning to have doubts. Although it seems that her marriage, sadly, has broken down, and that she is without a home, I cannot find any words which state clearly that she wishes to return. But there is something about the way she describes her memories of the house that is definitely nostalgic. It would not surprise me to discover that she would be happy to come back.

But again, why am I wasting time imagining what might or might not happen in the future? It will happen soon enough. And I have moved away from the subject of this evening's events. These last few hours, I have to say, have been very difficult for me. I am sure that my kind hosts, Mr and Mrs Taylor, did not deliberately intend to make me suffer. But as soon as I had sat down to supper at their table, a most uncomfortable situation began to develop.

♦

A large, rough wooden table dominated the room downstairs at the front of the cottage. On its surface there were many small marks left over the years by bread-knives and other sharp instruments. I could see them clearly despite the fact that the only light in the room came from an oil lamp on a shelf in one corner.

'We've been without electricity for almost two months,' Mr Taylor explained. 'But we don't miss it much. There are a few houses in the village that have never had electricity at all. Oil gives a warmer light.'

Mrs Taylor served us with a good soup, and I was looking forward to an hour or so of pleasant conversation before going to bed. However, just as we had finished supper and Mr Taylor was pouring me a glass of home-made beer, we heard footsteps on the stony path outside.

'I wonder who that is?' Mr Taylor said, a tone of mild curiosity in his voice.

'It's George Andrews,' a voice came from outside. 'I was just passing.'

The next moment a well-built, middle-aged man in farming clothes entered the room, and Mr and Mrs Taylor gave him a warm welcome. With the easy informality of a regular visitor, he sat down on a small chair by the doorway and removed his muddy boots. Then he came towards the table, stopped and stood in front of me like a soldier reporting to an officer.

'The name's Andrews, sir,' he said. 'A very good evening to you. I'm very sorry to hear about your problem, but I'm sure you'll be happy spending the night here in Moscombe.'

The fact that Mr Andrews had heard about my 'problem' puzzled me. But I replied with a smile that I was very grateful for the warm treatment I had received. I had of course been referring to Mr and Mrs Taylor's kindness, but Mr Andrews seemed to think that my expression of thanks included him because he immediately said:

'Oh no, sir, you're most welcome. We're very pleased to have you. We don't have gentlemen like you passing this way very often. We're all very pleased you could visit us.'

The way he said this seemed to suggest that the whole village was aware of my 'problem' and of my arrival at this cottage.

A few minutes later another visitor arrived. He looked and behaved so much like Mr Andrews that at first I thought they were brothers. But then the newcomer introduced himself to me as:

'Morgan, sir. Trevor Morgan.'

Mr Morgan expressed regret concerning my 'problem', and assured me that all would be well in the morning. He finished by saying:

'It's a privilege to have a gentleman like yourself here in Moscombe, sir.'

Before I could think of a reply to this, a middle-aged couple arrived and were introduced to me as Mr and Mrs Harry Smith. As they took their places around the table, Mr Harry Smith said:

'I believe that beautiful old Ford up there on Thornley Bush Hill, sir, is your car?'

I agreed, then added:

'But I'm surprised to hear you've seen it.'

'I've not seen it myself, sir. But Dave Thornton passed it on his tractor a short time ago as he was coming home. He was so surprised to see it there, he actually stopped and got out.' Then Mr Smith turned to the others around the table. 'It's an absolute beauty. Dave said he'd never seen a car like it.'

'Your health, sir,' somebody said, lifting a glass of beer, and everybody around the table drank to my health.

I smiled and said:

'I assure you, the privilege is all mine.'

'You're very kind, sir,' Mrs Smith said. 'You're a real gentleman.

Not like Mr Lindsay. He may have had a lot of money, but he was no gentleman.'

There was general agreement with this comment, and Mr Taylor explained by saying:

'Mr Lindsay used to live in the big house not far from here, sir. He wasn't very popular.'

Mrs Smith then leaned towards me and said:

'We told Doctor Carlisle you were here, sir. The doctor would be very pleased to meet you.'

'I expect he has patients to see,' Mrs Taylor added apologetically. 'I'm afraid we can't say for certain when he'll be here.'

Before I could reply, Mr Harry Smith leaned forward and said:

'That Mr Lindsay, he had it all wrong, see? Acting the way he did, thinking he was so wonderful. But he soon learnt his lesson.'

'He was no gentleman,' Mr Taylor agreed.

'That's right, sir,' Mr Harry Smith said. 'He had a fine house and good suits, but we could all tell he was no gentleman.'

'That's true,' Mr Taylor said. 'You can always tell a real gentleman. You, for example, sir. It's not just the style of your clothes, or your fine way of speaking. There's something else that shows you're a gentleman. Hard to say exactly what it is, but it's clear for everyone to see.'

There were more sounds of agreement around the table.

Mr Morgan, who had said little since his arrival, bent forward and said to me:

'What do you think it is, sir? Maybe someone who's got it has a better idea of what it is. We're all talking about who's got it and who hasn't, and we don't know what we're talking about. Perhaps you could tell us, sir?'

There was silence around the table and everybody looked at me. I gave a small cough and said:

'It is hardly for me to say what qualities I may or may not

possess. But in answer to your question, I suspect that the word you're looking for is dignity.'

'There's a lot of truth in that, sir,' Mr Andrews nodded, and a number of voices agreed with him.

But Harry Smith said:

'Excuse me for not agreeing with you completely, sir, but in my opinion dignity doesn't just belong to gentlemen. Dignity's something every man and woman in the country can get, if they try. Forgive me, sir, but we like to express our opinions directly around here.'

I decided that it would be too complicated to attempt to argue with him, so I just smiled and said:

'Of course, you're quite correct.'

Mr Harry Smith, however, had not finished. He leaned even further forward and began to talk about the war. In his opinion, everybody who fought Hitler was a hero. Every Englishman who risked his life in order to defend the country had an important part to play. There should be freedom of speech and dignity for all Englishmen, rich or poor. It didn't matter how poor or uneducated a person was. Everybody's opinion was important, and the government should pay attention to what people from villages like Moscombe wanted to say. Mr Taylor tried to interrupt, but nothing could stop Mr Harry Smith. After several minutes, he finished by saying:

'I'm not talking politics, sir. I'm just saying that you can't have dignity if you're a slave. That's why we fought Hitler. For the freedom to have dignity, however poor we might be.'

'This may seem like a small, unimportant place, sir,' his wife then added. 'But we lost many young men in the war.'

At this, the room went very quiet. Finally, Mr Taylor broke the silence by saying to me:

'Harry does a lot of organizing for our local member of parliament. He loves telling everybody what's wrong with the country.'

'Ah, but I was saying what's *right* about the country.' Mr Harry Smith attempted to start arguing again.

But Mr Andrews ignored him and asked me:

'Have you had any connection with politics yourself, sir?'

'Not directly,' I said. 'And certainly not these days. More before the war, perhaps.'

'It's just that I remember a Mr Stevens who was a member of parliament a couple of years ago. That wasn't you, was it, sir?'

'Oh no,' I said with a laugh.

I am not at all sure what made me make my next statement. I can only say that it seemed somehow appropriate to the circumstances. For then I said:

'In fact, I was more involved in international affairs than domestic ones.'

At these words, my listeners looked at me with a mixture of wonder and respect. I added quickly:

'Of course, I was never in government myself. I was only an unofficial adviser.' But they continued to stare at me quietly.

Finally Mrs Taylor broke the silence and said:

'Excuse me, sir, have you ever met Mr Churchill?'

'Mr Churchill? He did come to the house on a number of occasions. But frankly, Mrs Taylor, while I was involved in great affairs, Mr Churchill was not as important as he later became. People like Mr Eden and Lord Halifax were more frequent visitors in those days.'

'But you have actually met Mr Churchill, sir? That must have been a great honour.'

'I don't agree with many things Mr Churchill says,' Mr Harry Smith said, 'but he's a great man. It must have been an honour to discuss things with him.'

'It was, as you say, a privilege to be in such a great man's company,' I said. 'It is true that I have been very fortunate. I have met not only Mr Churchill, but also many other great men from

America and Europe. I have been very lucky to be able to advise such important people on the great topics of the day. I do feel most grateful for my good fortune.'

The conversation continued in this way for some time. I was asked about the famous people I had met, and Mr Harry Smith kept repeating how important it was for people 'in high places' to listen to the opinions of ordinary people like himself.

Suddenly his wife said:

'I wonder where Doctor Carlisle is. I'm sure the gentleman would appreciate some *educated* talk now.'

Everybody laughed. I decided the time was right for me to go to bed.

'Although it has been extremely enjoyable to meet you all,' I said, 'I must confess I'm beginning to feel a little tired . . .'

'Of course, sir,' Mrs Taylor said, 'you must be exhausted. Perhaps I'll fetch another blanket for you. It's getting much colder at night now.'

'No, I assure you, Mrs Taylor, I'll be perfectly comfortable.'

But before I could rise from the table, Mr Morgan said:

'Ah, there's someone coming. I expect that's the doctor.'

'I really must go,' I said. 'I feel quite exhausted.'

'But I'm sure this is the doctor now, sir,' said Mrs Smith. 'Do wait a few more minutes.'

Just as she said this, there was a knock on the door and a voice said:

'It's only me, Mrs Taylor.'

Doctor Carlisle was a tall, thin gentleman of about forty years old. No sooner had he said good evening to everybody than Mrs Taylor said to him:

'This is our gentleman here, Doctor. His car's stuck up at Thornley Bush and he's been having to listen to Harry's speeches as a result.'

The doctor came up to the table.

'Richard Carlisle,' he said with a cheerful smile as I rose to shake his hand. 'Bad luck about your car. Still, I hope you're being well looked after.'

'Thank you,' I replied. 'Everyone has been most kind.'

'Well, nice to have you with us.' Doctor Carlisle sat down directly opposite me. 'Which part of the country are you from?'

'Oxfordshire,' I said. Indeed, I found it hard to resist the urge to add 'sir'.

'I have an uncle who lives just outside Oxford. Fine part of the country.'

'The gentleman was just telling us, Doctor,' Mrs Smith said, 'that he knows Mr Churchill.'

'Really? I used to know a nephew of his, but we've lost touch. Never had the privilege of meeting the great man, though.'

'And not only Mr Churchill,' Mrs Smith went on. 'He knows Mr Eden and Lord Halifax.'

'Really?'

The doctor's eyes examined me closely. Before I could make an appropriate remark, however, Mr Andrews said to the doctor:

'The gentleman was telling us that before the war he was involved in foreign affairs.'

'Indeed?'

The doctor went on studying me for several seconds, then he regained his cheerful manner and asked:

'Touring around for pleasure?'

'Mainly,' I said, and gave a small laugh.

'Plenty of nice country around here.' Then he turned to talk to Mr Andrews about something he had borrowed and had not yet returned.

For a short time, I was no longer the centre of attention and I was able to remain silent. Then, at an appropriate moment, I rose to my feet and said:

'Please excuse me. It has been a most enjoyable evening, but I am really very tired.'

Mrs Smith and a few others tried to persuade me to stay, while Doctor Carlisle studied me closely. Eventually, however, I began to make my way around the table. To my embarrassment, everyone in the room, including Doctor Carlisle, rose to their feet. I thanked everybody again for their kindness and good company. I had almost left the room when the doctor's voice caused me to stop at the door.

'Mr Stevens, I have to go to Stanbury first thing in the morning. I'd be happy to give you a lift to your car. It will save you the walk. And we can pick up a can of petrol on the way.'

'That's most kind,' I said. 'But I don't wish to put you to any trouble.'

'No trouble at all. Seven thirty all right for you?'

'That would be most helpful, thank you.'

There was another exchange of goodnights, and I was at last allowed to withdraw to my room.

Chapter 14   Dignity

I feel very uncomfortable about what has just happened, but I don't know how I could have prevented the misunderstanding regarding my identity. By the time I was aware of what was happening, things had already gone too far. I could not have told these people the truth without much embarrassment. On the other hand, I do not see that any real harm has been done. I will, after all, be leaving these people in the morning and will probably never meet them again. I ought to stop worrying myself about the matter.

However, apart from the unfortunate misunderstanding, there is something else about this evening that deserves some thought: Mr Harry Smith's comments regarding the nature of 'dignity'.

There is, I suppose, some truth in the idea that poor people are as capable of dignity as rich people. Perhaps everybody in the land has a duty to think about the important matters of the day. But in reality, how can ordinary people be expected to have 'strong opinions' on everything – as Mr Harry Smith believes that the villagers here do? In my opinion, these expectations are not only impossible but also undesirable. There is, after all, a real limit to how much ordinary people can learn and know. It cannot be wise, surely, to expect every single person to be able to contribute 'strong opinions' to the great debates of the nation.

I remember an instance which illustrates the limitations of Mr Harry Smith's arguments rather well. It occurred before the war, around 1935.

Very late one night, I was called to the drawing room, where his lordship had been entertaining three gentlemen since dinner. I had, of course, been called to the drawing room many times that evening. On each occasion, the three gentlemen had been deep in serious conversation. When I entered the drawing room on this last occasion, however, all the gentlemen stopped talking and looked at me. Then his lordship said:

'Step this way a moment, will you, Stevens? Mr Spencer here wishes to have a word with you.'

Mr Spencer looked at me for a moment from his armchair, then said:

'My good man, I have a question for you. We need your help on a certain topic that we've been debating. Tell me, do you think our debts to America are responsible for the present low levels of trade?'

I was naturally a little surprised by this, but then quickly understood the situation. The gentleman clearly expected me to be puzzled by his question. It took me a moment or two to realize what was happening, but in that time I must have given the wrong impression. The gentlemen in the room probably thought that I was trying to think of an answer to the question, for I saw them all exchange amused smiles.

'I'm very sorry, sir,' I said, 'but I am unable to be of assistance on this matter.'

I was by now in control of the situation, but the gentlemen went on smiling. Then Mr Spencer said:

'Then perhaps you will help us with another matter. Do you think that the economic problems in Europe would improve if there was a military agreement between France and Russia?'

'I'm very sorry, sir, but I am unable to be of assistance on this matter either.'

'Oh dear,' said Mr Spencer. 'So you can't help us.'

There was more quiet laughter, then his lordship said:

'Thank you, Stevens. That is all.'

But Mr Spencer had not finished. 'Please, Darlington,' he said. 'I have one more question to ask your good man here. I very much wanted his advice concerning a problem that has been bothering us all recently. My good fellow, please help us. What was Monsieur Laval really intending when he made his recent speech about North Africa?'

'I'm sorry, sir, but I am unable to assist in this matter.'

'You see, gentleman,' Mr Spencer turned to the others and said, 'our man is unable to assist us in these matters.'

The laughter became louder, and he went on:

'But we still continue with the ridiculous belief that our good man here, and a few million others like him, should decide how to run the country. With a parliamentary system like ours, I'm not surprised that we never seem able to find solutions to any of our problems. It would be just as good to ask the mothers' union to organize a war.'

There was open laughter at this comment, during which his lordship said quietly:

'Thank you, Stevens. That is all.'

The following morning his lordship came into the games room, where I was dusting the paintings, and said:

'I'm sorry, Stevens. We were awful to you last night.'

'Not at all, sir,' I said from the top of my stepladder. 'I was only happy to be of service.'

'It was terrible. I think we'd all had too much to drink. Please accept my apologies.'

'Thank you, sir. But I am happy to assure you I was not offended at all.'

His lordship walked over to a leather armchair and sat down with a tired look on his face. For a while he stared out of the windows at the winter sunshine over the hills. I looked down from my stepladder and was suddenly aware of how much his lordship had changed in recent years. The pressures of life had had a great effect on him. He had become extremely thin, his hair had gone completely white and there were deep lines on his face.

Suddenly, his lordship spoke. 'You must understand, Stevens, we're making terrible mistakes in this country. If it's any comfort to you, last night you did contribute to our discussion. There's too much nonsense nowadays about ordinary people telling the government what to do.'

'Indeed, sir.'

'We're really too slow in this country to recognize when something's out of date. Other great nations have recognized the fact that change is needed. But our country...' Lord Darlington stared in silence at the view from the window for a moment, and sadly shook his head. 'Our country is always the last to change. One day soon, we'll need to accept the fact that democracy is old-fashioned and doesn't work in today's complicated world.'

'The nation does seem to be in a regrettable condition, sir,' I said.

'Absolutely, Stevens. Look at Germany and Italy. See what strong leadership can achieve if they're free to act. No democratic nonsense there. If your house is on fire, you don't call the staff into the drawing room and discuss the best method of escape for an hour, do you?'

As I remember these words, it occurs to me that many of Lord Darlington's ideas probably seem rather odd today – perhaps even unattractive. But there is surely some truth in what he said to me that morning in the games room. Of course, it is ridiculous to expect a butler to answer the sort of questions that Mr Spencer asked me that night. It is clearly nonsense, therefore, for Mr Harry Smith to say that people can only have dignity if their voices are heard in high places. The fact is, the great affairs of the nation will always be too complicated for people like you and me to understand. Only great gentlemen like Lord Darlington can decide what is right and what is not right for our country. It is the duty of the rest of us to serve these gentlemen to the best of our ability.

Throughout the years I served him, Lord Darlington always made all the important decisions. I was not expected to offer him advice or judgement. It was my duty to be loyal to him, and not to worry about whether he was right or wrong. I was devoted to him and I performed my duties as well as I was able. Indeed, many may consider my performance of my duties to have been 'first class'. It is hardly my fault if many people now believe that his lordship's life and work were a sad waste. The passage of time may now show that some of Lord Darlington's efforts were foolish, but I have no regrets about my part in things. It is illogical for me to feel any shame.

Chapter 15   The Rose Garden Hotel

1956

I have finally arrived at Little Compton, in Cornwall. I have recently finished lunch and am now sitting in the dining hall of the Rose Garden Hotel. Outside, the rain is falling steadily.

I have spent much of the past hour watching the rain falling on the village square. I have considered leaving now to meet Miss Kenton, but in my letter I informed her that I would see her at three o'clock. I do not want to surprise her by arriving too early. If the rain does not stop, I shall probably remain here and drink tea until the proper time for me to go.

I am surprised that it is raining, because the sun was shining brightly this morning when I got up. Mrs Taylor cooked me a fine breakfast of farm eggs and toast, and Doctor Carlisle called for me at seven thirty, as he had promised.

'I found a can of petrol for you,' he announced as soon as I had said goodbye to the Taylors. I thanked him and offered to pay, but he refused to accept my money.

'Nonsense,' he said. 'It's just enough for you to reach the next village. They have a proper garage there.'

I sat in the passenger seat of Doctor Carlisle's car as he drove out of the village and up a narrow road between tall trees. After asking me how I had slept at the Taylors, he said quite suddenly:

'I hope you don't think I'm being rude. But you aren't a manservant by any chance, are you?'

I must confess, I felt some relief when I heard this question.

'I am indeed, sir. In fact, I am the butler of Darlington Hall, near Oxford.'

'I thought so. When I heard that you had met Winston Churchill, I thought that you were either lying or that you must be a kind of servant.'

He turned to me with a friendly smile, and I said:

'It was not my intention to deceive anyone, sir. However . . .'

'Oh, there's no need to explain. I can see how it happened. I mean, the people around here are sure to think you're at least a lord.' The doctor laughed loudly. 'It's probably good to be mistaken for a lord from time to time.'

We travelled in silence for a few moments, then Doctor Carlisle said to me:

'Well, I hope you enjoyed your little stay with us here.'

'I did very much, thank you, sir.'

'I wish you wouldn't call me "sir" all the time, Mr Stevens. Now this road should be familiar to you. Probably looks rather different in the daylight. Is that the car there? What a handsome vehicle!'

Doctor Carlisle stopped just behind the Ford, got out and said again:

'What a handsome vehicle.' Then he quickly produced the can of petrol and kindly filled the tank of the Ford for me. When I sat once again in the driving seat and turned the key, the engine came to life. I thanked Doctor Carlisle and we said goodbye to each other. I followed his car along the twisting hill road for two or three kilometres, and then he turned off towards Stanbury and I was alone again.

I crossed the border into Cornwall at about nine o'clock. This was three hours before the rain began, and the clouds were still a brilliant white. In fact, the scenery was some of the most beautiful I had ever seen. Unfortunately, I did not pay it the attention it deserved, because I was thinking for most of the time about Miss Kenton. Before the end of the day, I kept thinking, I would be meeting her again for the first time in twenty years.

And now, as I sit here in Little Compton, watching the rain as it splashes on the pavements of the village square outside, my mind keeps returning to the past. I have been thinking about one thing in particular all morning.

I remember standing alone in the corridor outside Miss Kenton's room. I was standing half turned towards her door, wondering whether or not I should knock. For some reason I was sure that behind that door, just a few metres away from me, Miss Kenton was crying. As I stood there, a very strange feeling rose inside me. I can't remember exactly why I was standing there. I suggested earlier that this might have been just after Miss Kenton received news of her aunt's death. But now, having thought more about it, I believe I may have been a little confused about this matter. I think it is more likely that this incident took place one evening a few months later. It was the evening when the young Mr Cardinal arrived at Darlington Hall rather unexpectedly.

Chapter 16   Events of International Significance

1936

Mr Cardinal's father, a close friend and colleague of his lordship's for many years, had been tragically killed in a riding accident three or four years earlier. Meanwhile, young Mr Cardinal had become a journalist famous for his funny, clever articles on international affairs.

Lord Darlington did not like Mr Cardinal's articles very much. He often used to look up from his newspaper and say something like:

'Young Reggie's writing such nonsense again. I'm glad his father's not alive to read this.'

But Mr Cardinal's articles did not prevent him from being a frequent visitor at the house. Indeed, his lordship treated him like a member of his own family, although Mr Cardinal still always gave prior warning of his visits. That evening, therefore, I was a little surprised when I answered the door and saw him standing there.

'Oh, hello, Stevens, how are you?' he said. 'I was just wondering if I could stay for the night. I've got a bit of a problem, I'm afraid.'

'It is very nice to see you again, sir. I shall tell his lordship you are here.'

'I had intended to stay at Mr Roland's place, but there's been a misunderstanding and they've gone away somewhere. I hope it's not too inconvenient. I mean, there aren't any special arrangements for tonight, are there?'

'I believe, sir, that his lordship is expecting some gentlemen to call after dinner.'

'Oh, that's bad luck. I seem to have chosen a bad night. I'd better stay out of the way, I think. I've got some work to do, anyway.'

'I shall tell his lordship that you are here, sir. You are in good time to join him for dinner.'

I left Mr Cardinal in the drawing room and made my way to the study, where his lordship was working on some papers. When I told him of Mr Cardinal's arrival, a look of surprised annoyance crossed his face. Then he leaned back in his chair with a deep frown.

'Tell Mr Cardinal I'll be down soon,' he said finally.

When I returned downstairs, I discovered Mr Cardinal walking around the drawing room. He seemed rather nervous. I gave him his lordship's message and asked him if he would like some refreshments.

'Just some tea, thank you, Stevens. Who is his lordship expecting tonight?'

'I'm sorry, sir. I'm afraid I'm unable to tell you.'

'No idea at all?'

'I'm sorry, sir.'

'Hmm, interesting. Oh well, I'd better stay out of the way.'

Soon afterwards, I went down to Miss Kenton's room. She was sitting at her table, although there was nothing in front of her and her hands were empty. Indeed, something about her suggested that she had been sitting like that for some time.

'Mr Cardinal is here, Miss Kenton,' I said. 'He'll require his usual room tonight.'

'Very well, Mr Stevens. I shall prepare it before I leave.'

'Ah, you are going out this evening, Miss Kenton?'

'I am indeed, Mr Stevens.'

Perhaps I looked a little surprised, for she went on:

'You will recall, Mr Stevens, that we discussed this a fortnight ago.'

'Yes, of course, Miss Kenton. I beg your pardon. I had forgotten.'

'Is something the matter, Mr Stevens?'

'Not at all, Miss Kenton. Some visitors are expected this evening, but your presence will not be required.'

'We agreed a fortnight ago, Mr Stevens, that I could have this evening off.'

'Of course, Miss Kenton. I do beg your pardon.'

I turned to leave, but then I was stopped at the door by Miss Kenton saying:

'Mr Stevens, I have something to tell you.'

'Yes, Miss Kenton?'

'It is about my friend, whom I am going to meet tonight.'

'Yes, Miss Kenton.'

'He has asked me to marry him. I thought I ought to tell you.'

'Indeed, Miss Kenton. That is very interesting.'

'I have not made up my mind yet. He starts a new job in the West Country next month. As I say, I haven't decided yet. But I thought you should be informed of the situation.'

'I'm very grateful, Miss Kenton. I do hope you have a pleasant evening. Now please excuse me.'

I met Miss Kenton again about twenty minutes later. I was halfway up the back stairs carrying a heavy tray when I heard the sound of angry footsteps on the floor below me. Turning, I saw Miss Kenton staring up at me from the foot of the stairs.

'Mr Stevens, do I understand that you wish me to remain on duty this evening?'

'Not at all, Miss Kenton. As you explained, you did inform me of your intentions some time ago.'

'But I can see you are very unhappy about my absence tonight.'

'Not at all, Miss Kenton.'

'Then why are you making so much noise in the kitchen? And why do you keep marching up and down the corridor outside my room? Were you hoping to make me change my mind?'

'Miss Kenton, the slight excitement in the kitchen is only because Mr Cardinal has come to dinner. There is absolutely no reason why you should not go out this evening.'

'I intend to go out, Mr Stevens. I wish to make this clear. I made arrangements weeks ago.'

'Indeed, Miss Kenton. And once again, I wish you a very pleasant evening.'

There was an odd atmosphere at dinner that evening between the two gentlemen. For long moments, they ate in silence. During one of these silences, Mr Cardinal said:

'Something special tonight, sir?'

'Eh?'

'Your visitors this evening. Special?'

'I'm afraid I can't tell you, my boy.'

'Oh dear. I suppose this means I can't join you.'

'Join me in what?'

'Whatever's taking place tonight.'

'Oh, it wouldn't interest you. Besides, it's private. And you're a journalist.'

After dinner, the gentlemen went into the smoking room. However, in contrast to their quiet mood at dinner, they soon began to exchange angry words with each other. Of course, I did not stop to listen, but I could not avoid hearing his lordship shouting:

'But that's not your business, my boy! Not your business!'

I was in the dining room when the two gentlemen eventually came out. They seemed calmer. As they crossed the hall, his lordship turned to Mr Cardinal and said:

'Now remember, my boy. I'm trusting you.'

'Yes, yes,' Mr Cardinal said with some annoyance. 'I promise.'

At eight thirty, I heard the sound of motors outside. I opened the door to a policeman. Over his shoulder I could see that other policemen with guns were moving off in different directions. The next moment, I was showing two very important gentlemen into the hall, where they were met by his lordship. He quickly took them into the drawing room.

Ten minutes later there was the sound of another car and I opened the door to Herr Ribbentrop, the German Ambassador. He, too, disappeared quickly into the drawing room. A few minutes later, when I was called in to provide refreshments, the four gentlemen were discussing sausages. The atmosphere seemed, on the surface, quite friendly.

After serving the four gentlemen with drinks, I went to my position near the entrance in the hall. I had been standing there for two hours when the back doorbell was rung. When I went down, I discovered a policeman standing there with Miss Kenton. He asked me to confirm her identity. Minutes later, as I was shutting the door, I noticed Miss Kenton waiting for me, and said:

'I hope you had a pleasant evening, Miss Kenton.'

She made no reply, so I repeated my comment as we were crossing the floor of the unlit kitchen.

'I did, thank you, Mr Stevens,' she said at last.

'I'm pleased to hear that.'

Behind me, Miss Kenton's footsteps suddenly stopped, and I heard her say:

'Are you not at all interested in what took place between my friend and me, Mr Stevens?'

83

'I do not mean to be rude, Miss Kenton, but I really must return upstairs immediately. Events of international significance are taking place in this house.'

'Very well, Mr Stevens. As you are in such a hurry, I shall be brief. I have accepted my friend's proposal of marriage.'

'Really, Miss Kenton? Then may I offer you my congratulations.'

'Thank you, Mr Stevens. Of course, I will not break my contract, but I would be very grateful if you could release me earlier. My friend begins his new job in the West Country in two weeks' time.'

'I will do my best to find a replacement at the earliest opportunity, Miss Kenton,' I said. 'Now please excuse me. I must return upstairs.'

I started to walk away again but, just as I had reached the door, I heard Miss Kenton's voice. 'Mr Stevens,' she said, her voice echoing strangely in the dark and empty kitchen. 'After the many years of service I have given in this house, is that all you have to say?'

'Miss Kenton, you have my warmest congratulations. But I repeat, there are matters of international importance taking place upstairs, and I must return immediately.'

'Did you know, Mr Stevens, that you have been a very important figure for my friend and me?'

'Really, Miss Kenton?'

'Yes, Mr Stevens. We often amuse ourselves with little stories about you.'

'Indeed, Miss Kenton. Now please excuse me.'

I went up to the hall and returned to my position by the main door. However, five minutes later, Mr Cardinal appeared in the doorway of the library and signalled for me to come over.

'Hate to bother you, Stevens,' he said. 'But could you possibly fetch me a little more whisky? The bottle you brought in earlier seems to be finished.'

84

'You are very welcome to whatever refreshments you desire, sir. However, as you have some work to do, I wonder whether another bottle is a good idea?'

'My work will be fine, Stevens. So be a good fellow and get me another bottle.'

'Very well, sir.'

When I returned to the library a moment later, Mr Cardinal was wandering around, reading the names of books on the shelves. As I approached, he sat down heavily into a leather armchair. I went over to him, poured a little whisky and gave him the glass.

'You know, Stevens, we've been friends for some time, haven't we?'

'Indeed, sir.'

'I always look forward to a little chat with you whenever I come here. Would you like to join me in a little drink?'

I politely refused his kind invitation, but Mr Cardinal insisted. 'I do wish you'd sit down, Stevens. I want us to talk as friends.'

'I'm sorry, sir.' I put down my tray and sat down – in an appropriate fashion – in the armchair that Mr Cardinal was indicating.

'That's better,' Mr Cardinal said. 'Now, Stevens, I really ought to be truthful with you. As you have probably guessed, I didn't come here tonight by accident. Somebody told me about what's going on here. I don't suppose you can tell me whether the Prime Minister's here, can you?'

'The Prime Minister, sir?'

'Oh, it's all right, you don't have to tell me. I understand you're in a difficult position.' He looked away tiredly for a moment towards his papers, which were scattered over the desk. Then he turned to me again and said:

'You know, Stevens, his lordship's been like a second father to me. I care for him very deeply. But we must face facts. He's in

85

trouble, and I'm extremely worried about him. He's dealing with very powerful people here, and he doesn't really understand what's going on.'

'Really, sir?'

'Stevens, do you know what's happening at this exact moment in that room across the hall? There are four men in that room – I don't need you to confirm it. His lordship, the British Prime Minister, the head of the Foreign Office and the German Ambassador. His lordship has worked hard for this meeting, and he genuinely believes he's doing something good and honourable. Do you know why his lordship has brought these gentlemen here tonight?'

'I'm afraid not, sir.'

'Tell me, Stevens, don't you care at all? Aren't you curious?'

'I do not believe that I am not curious, sir. However, it is not my job to display curiosity about such matters.'

'I suppose you think that's being loyal? To his lordship? Or to the King?'

'I'm sorry, sir. I fail to understand what you are proposing.'

Mr Cardinal shook his head sadly. 'I'm not proposing anything, Stevens. Quite frankly, I don't know what we can do. But I wish you would be more curious.'

He was silent for a moment and seemed to be staring emptily at the area of carpet around my feet. Finally he looked up and said:

'Are you sure you won't join me in a drink, Stevens?'

'No thank you, sir.'

'The fact is, Stevens, his lordship doesn't realize what's happening. He's become Herr Hitler's puppet. Have you noticed what's been happening over the last three or four years?'

'I'm sorry, sir, I'm afraid I have not.'

'Of course not, Stevens. You're not curious. The problem is, Stevens,' Mr Cardinal said, moving into a more upright position in his armchair, 'his lordship is a true, old English gentleman. He feels it is honourable to offer generosity and friendship to a defeated enemy. But they're using him, Stevens – the Nazis are using him to help them achieve their own terrible aims. Do you remember that American senator all those years ago? He said the world was too complicated for true gentlemen. Well, he was right. You've seen how they have used his lordship, haven't you, Stevens?'

'I'm sorry, sir, but I cannot say that I have.'

'Well, I don't know about you, Stevens, but I'm going to do something about it. If Father were alive, he would do something to stop it. You have no idea what they're discussing in that room across the hall, Stevens? Then I'll tell you. His lordship has been trying to persuade the Prime Minister to accept an invitation to visit Herr Hitler. And that is not all, Stevens. His lordship is discussing the possibility of a royal visit to Germany. Everybody knows the new king has always been enthusiastic about the Nazis. Well, apparently he's keen to accept Herr Hitler's invitation. His lordship is now trying to persuade the British government to agree to this awful idea.'

'I'm sorry, sir, but I have to say that I trust his lordship's judgement completely.'

At that moment I heard the bell from the drawing room. I asked Mr Cardinal to excuse me, and I left the room.

In the drawing room, the air was thick with tobacco smoke. The gentlemen sat and smoked in silence, while his lordship asked me to bring up a bottle of wine from the cellar. As I was making my way along the darkness of the corridor towards the cellar, the door to Miss Kenton's room suddenly opened.

'I am surprised to find you still awake, Miss Kenton,' I said when I saw her in the doorway.

'Mr Stevens, I was very foolish earlier,' she said.

'Excuse me, Miss Kenton, but I have no time to talk just now.'

'Mr Stevens, you must not take anything I said earlier seriously. I was simply being foolish.'

'Miss Kenton, I cannot remember what you may be referring to. Besides, events of great importance are developing upstairs, and I cannot stop to chat with you. I suggest that you go to bed.'

With that, I hurried on. It did not take me long to find the bottle in the cellar. Just a few minutes after my brief meeting with Miss Kenton, I was walking along the corridor again on my return journey. As I approached Miss Kenton's door, I saw from the light around its edges that she was still awake. And that was the moment, I am now sure, that has remained clearly in my memory to this day. At that moment, as I paused in the darkness of the corridor, a tray in my hands, something told me that just a few metres away, on the other side of the door, Miss Kenton was crying. I do not know why I was so sure of this. I had certainly not heard any sounds of crying.

I do not know how long I remained standing there. At the time it seemed a significant period, but in reality it was probably only a few seconds. For, of course, I was required to hurry upstairs to serve some of the most important gentlemen in Europe. I'm sure that I would not have delayed there for long.

After serving the gentlemen in the drawing room, I returned to my position in the hall. I stood there for another hour until the gentlemen finally departed. As I stood there, a strange thing began to happen. I began to experience a deep feeling of pride. I had, after all, just come through an extremely difficult evening, throughout which I had managed to preserve my dignity. My father would have been proud of the way I had performed my duty that night.

Chapter 17   Old Friends

September 1956

For many years I have often thought of visiting the seaside town of Weymouth. I have heard various people talk of pleasant holidays here. All of them mentioned the pier in particular, and I have been walking up and down along it for the last half-hour. They especially recommended visiting the pier in the evening, when it becomes lit up with bulbs of various colours. A moment ago, I learnt from an official that the lights would be switched on soon, so I have decided to sit down here on this bench and wait for them to come on. I have a good view of the sun setting over the sea. Although there is still plenty of daylight left – it has been a splendid day – I can see, here and there, lights starting to come on all along the shore.

I arrived in this town yesterday afternoon, and have decided to remain here for a second night. I need a rest from motoring, and if I make an early start tomorrow, I shall be back at Darlington Hall by tea-time.

It is now two days since my meeting with Miss Kenton in the tea lounge of the Rose Garden Hotel in Little Compton. Miss Kenton surprised me by coming to the hotel. I was looking out of the window at the rain when a member of the hotel staff came to inform me that a lady wished to see me at reception. I rose and left the dining hall, but at reception I was told that the lady had gone into the tea lounge.

The tea lounge was empty apart from Miss Kenton. She rose as I entered, smiled and held out her hand to me.

'Ah, Mr Stevens. How nice to see you again.'

'Mrs Benn, how lovely.'

We moved two armchairs close to the window, and sat and talked for the next two hours. While we talked together, the rain continued to fall steadily on the square outside. A grey light from the window fell across her face, and I noticed the lines around her eyes and mouth. But, on the whole, Miss Kenton looked surprisingly similar to the person I remembered from twenty years ago. It was a great pleasure for me to see her again.

For the first twenty minutes we chatted politely about my

journey. As we talked, I began to notice other ways in which Miss Kenton had changed since I last saw her. For instance, she appeared, somehow, *slower*. It is possible that this was simply the calmness that comes with age, but I could not help thinking that it was more a sort of tiredness with life. Every now and then, when she was not speaking, I thought I saw something like sadness in her expression. But I may have been mistaken about this.

The initial awkwardness of our conversation soon developed into something more relaxed and personal. We spent some time remembering various people from the past, or exchanging recent news about them. This was, I must say, most enjoyable. As we talked, the past began to come back to life for me. It was not just the memory of people and places that we talked about. I watched Miss Kenton while she was speaking, and suddenly recognized little expressions on her face, little movements of her hands, that brought back memories of our conversations all those years ago. The little smile that she gave when she finished speaking, and a certain gesture with her shoulders, had not changed at all.

After we had talked about people we had once known, Miss Kenton began to tell me about herself. I learnt, for instance, that her marriage to Mr Benn was not in as much trouble as I had understood from her letter. Although she had left her home for a period of four or five days – which was when she had written me her letter – she had returned, and Mr Benn had been very pleased to have her back. 'It is fortunate that one of us is sensible about these things,' she said with a smile.

I am, of course, aware that details of Miss Kenton's personal life with her husband were really not my business. I would not have talked to her about such private matters if there had not been an important professional reason. And my reason for encouraging conversation on this subject was the present staffing problem at Darlington Hall. But Miss Kenton did not seem to mind talking to me about these matters. In my opinion, this is pleasing evidence of the fact that we had once enjoyed a close working relationship together.

For a short time, Miss Kenton went on talking more generally about her husband, who is retiring soon because of ill health. She also talked to me about her daughter, who is now married and expecting a child in the autumn. In fact, Miss Kenton gave me her daughter's address in Dorset. 'Catherine's heard all about you, Mr Stevens,' she said. 'She'd be so thrilled to meet you.'

Then I began to tell her about myself. I tried to describe to her what Darlington Hall is like today. I attempted to tell her what a good employer Mr Farraday is, and I described the changes to the house itself and the present staffing arrangements. Miss Kenton, I thought, became visibly happier when I talked about the house, and we were soon laughing again together over various old memories.

I spoke about Lord Darlington only once. We had been talking about the young Mr Cardinal, and I had to tell Miss Kenton that he had been tragically killed in Belgium during the war. I continued:

'Of course, his lordship was very fond of Mr Cardinal. He suffered very badly when the young man died.'

I did not wish to spoil the pleasant atmosphere with unhappy talk, so I quickly tried to change the subject. However, Miss Kenton wanted to hear more about Lord Darlington. She had read in the newspapers about his unsuccessful court action and, inevitably, took the opportunity to ask me about it.

'The fact is, Mrs Benn, throughout the war, people said some truly terrible things about his lordship. The newspaper that young Mr Cardinal worked for was especially vicious towards him. His lordship did nothing about it while the country was in danger, but the accusations against him continued after the war had ended. He was unable to continue suffering in silence. His lordship sincerely believed that he would get justice if he took that newspaper to court. Instead, of course, the newspaper simply became more popular, and his lordship's good name was destroyed for ever. Afterwards, his lordship became very ill. The house became so quiet. I would take him tea in the drawing room and, well . . . it really was most tragic to see.'

'I'm very sorry, Mr Stevens. I had no idea things had been so bad.'

'Oh yes, Mrs Benn. But enough of this. I know you remember Darlington Hall in the days when it was filled with important visitors. That is how his lordship deserves to be remembered.'

We did not mention Lord Darlington again. We talked for the rest of the time about happy memories, and we spent an extremely pleasant two hours together in the tea lounge of the Rose Garden Hotel. Indeed, I could hardly believe that two whole hours had passed when Miss Kenton looked up at the clock and said that she would have to return home. When I discovered that she would have to walk in the rain to a bus stop just outside the village, I insisted on taking her there in the Ford.

Soon we were motoring together down the village high street, past the shops, and out into the open country. Miss Kenton sat quietly watching the passing view, then turned to me and said:

'Why are you smiling to yourself like that, Mr Stevens?'

'Oh . . . You must excuse me, Mrs Benn, but I was just thinking about some of the things you wrote in your letter. I was a little worried when I read them, but I see now that there was no cause for alarm.'

'Oh? What things in particular are you referring to, Mr Stevens?'

'Well, for instance, Mrs Benn,' I said with a laugh, 'in one part of your letter you write: *The rest of my life stretches out emptily before me.* Or something like that.'

'Really, Mr Stevens,' she said, also laughing a little. 'I could not have written that.'

'I assure you, Mrs Benn, you did. I recall it very clearly.'

'Oh dear. Well, perhaps there are some days when I feel like that. But they pass quickly enough. Let me assure you, Mr Stevens, my life does not stretch out emptily before me. For instance, my husband and I are both looking forward to becoming grandparents.'

'Yes, indeed. That will be splendid for you.'

We drove on quietly for a few moments. Then Miss Kenton said:

'And what about you, Mr Stevens? What does the future hold for you back at Darlington Hall?'

'There is work, Mrs Benn. Work and more work. I wish I had some emptiness to look forward to.'

We both laughed at this. Then Miss Kenton pointed to a bus shelter further along the road. As we approached it, she said:

'Will you wait with me, Mr Stevens? The bus will only be a few minutes.'

The rain was still falling steadily as we got out of the car and hurried towards the shelter. Miss Kenton sat on the seat that was provided. I, however, remained on my feet where I would have a clear view of the approaching bus. After we had been waiting in silence for a few minutes, I finally managed to say:

'Excuse me, Mrs Benn. But the fact is, we may not meet again for a long time. I wonder if you would perhaps permit me to ask you a rather personal question. It is something that has been bothering me for some time.'

'Certainly, Mr Stevens. We are old friends, after all.'

'Indeed, as you say, we are old friends. Please do not reply if you feel you shouldn't. But the fact is, over the years I have had a number of letters from you, and they have all seemed to suggest that you are – how might one express it? – rather unhappy. I simply wondered if you were being badly treated in some way. Forgive me, but I have been worried about this for some time.'

'Mr Stevens, there is no need to be so embarrassed. We are old friends after all, are we not? In fact, I'm very grateful that you are so concerned. And I can reassure you on this matter absolutely. My husband does not treat me badly in any way. He is not a cruel or bad-tempered man at all.'

'I am so pleased to hear that, Mrs Benn.'

I leaned forward into the rain, looking for signs of the bus.

'I can see you are not very satisfied, Mr Stevens,' Miss Kenton said. 'Don't you believe me?'

'It's not that, Mrs Benn. Not that at all. It's just that you do not seem to have been very happy over the years. You have – forgive me – left your husband a number of times. If he does not treat you badly, then, well . . . I find the cause of your unhappiness rather difficult to understand.'

I looked out into the rain again. Eventually, I heard Miss Kenton say behind me:

'Mr Stevens, how can I explain? I hardly know myself why I do such things. But it is true, I have left him three times.' She paused a moment while I continued to look out towards the fields on the other side of the road. Then she said:

'I suppose, Mr Stevens, you're asking whether or not I love my husband.'

'Really, Mrs Benn, I would never . . .'

'I feel I should answer you, Mr Stevens,' Mrs Benn interrupted me. 'As you say, we may not meet again for many years. Yes, I do love my husband. I did not at first. I did not for a long time. When I left Darlington Hall all those years ago, I never realized I was really, truly leaving. I believe I thought of it, Mr Stevens, as simply another way to annoy you. It was a shock to come out here and find myself married. For a long time I was very unhappy, very unhappy indeed. But then the years passed, there was the war and Catherine grew up. Then suddenly, one day, I realized that I loved my husband. If you spend so much time with someone, you get used to him. He is a kind, steady man, and yes, Mr Stevens, I do love him.'

Miss Kenton fell silent again for a moment. Then she went on:

'But there are times, of course, when one thinks to oneself: "What a terrible mistake I have made with my life." And one thinks about a different life, a *better* life one might have had. For instance, I started to think about a life I might have had with you, Mr Stevens. And I suppose that is when I get angry over something small and unimportant and leave. But I always return to my husband. We cannot turn the clock back now. We cannot spend our lives dreaming about what might have been. One should be grateful for what one has.'

I do not think I responded immediately, for it took me a moment or two to fully understand her words. Moreover, the implication of Miss Kenton's words did create a certain amount of sorrow within me. Indeed – why should I not admit it? – at that moment, my heart was breaking. Before long, however, I turned to her and said with a smile:

'You are absolutely right, Mrs Benn. As you say, it is too late to turn back the clock. We must both be grateful for what we *do* have. And from what you tell me, Mrs Benn, you have many good reasons for feeling happy. In fact, it seems that you and Mr Benn have some extremely happy years ahead of you. You really must not let any more foolish ideas come between yourself and the happiness you deserve.'

'Of course, you are right, Mr Stevens. You are so kind.'

'Ah, Mrs Benn, I think that the bus is coming now.'

I stepped out into the rain and signalled, while Miss Kenton stood up and waited at the edge of the shelter. As the bus slowed down, I glanced at Miss Kenton and noticed that her eyes had filled with tears. I smiled and said:

'Now, Mrs Benn, you must take good care of yourself. Many people say that retirement is the best part of life for a married couple. You must make these years happy ones for yourself and your husband. We may never meet again, Mrs Benn, so I ask you to remember what I have just said to you.'

'I will, Mr Stevens, thank you. And thank you for the lift. It was so very kind of you. It was so nice to see you again.'

'It was a great pleasure to see you again, Mrs Benn.'

Chapter 18   The Best Part of the Day

The pier lights have been switched on, and a crowd of people behind me have just given a loud cheer to celebrate this event. There is still plenty of daylight left – the sky over the sea has turned a pale red – but it seems to me that everybody on this pier will be happy for night to fall. This confirms something that the man who was next to me on this bench said to me a short time ago. He claimed that, for many people, the evening was the best part of the day. It was the part of the day that they most looked forward to. There seems to be some truth in this. Otherwise, why would people cheer so loudly simply because the pier lights have come on?

The man had been sitting next to me for some minutes before I noticed him. I was so lost in my own thoughts that I did not know he was there until he said:

'Sea air is very good for you.'

He was a heavily built man in his late sixties, wearing an old brown jacket and an open-necked shirt. He was staring out across the water, so I was not sure whether he was talking to me. But since no one else responded, I eventually said:

'Yes, I'm sure it is.'

'The doctor says it's good for you, so I come up here as often as I can.'

The man went on to tell me about his various illnesses. He

turned to me occasionally and gave me a nod or a grin, but most of the time he kept staring out to sea. I only really started to pay him attention, however, when he mentioned that he had once been a butler. Until he retired three years ago, he had been the butler in a small house near Weymouth. He had been the only full-time member of staff. When I asked him if he had ever worked with a proper staff under him, perhaps before the war, he replied:

'Oh, in those days I was just a footman. I didn't have enough experience to be a butler in *those* days. Being a butler was a difficult job in those big houses before the war.'

When he told me this, I thought it was appropriate to reveal my identity. My companion seemed suitably impressed when I mentioned Darlington Hall.

'And I was trying to explain the job to *you*,' he said with a laugh. 'You never know who you're talking to when you meet a stranger. So you had a big staff, I suppose. Before the war, I mean.'

He was a cheerful fellow, and seemed genuinely interested, so I was happy to tell him about Darlington Hall in the old days. Eventually, I said:

'Of course, things are quite different today under my present employer. An American gentleman.'

'Americans are the ones who can afford it now,' he said, giving me a little grin.

'Yes,' I said, laughing a little. 'That's true.'

The man turned back to the sea again and took a deep breath. We sat quietly for several moments.

'The fact is, of course,' I said after a while, 'I gave my best to Lord Darlington. I gave him the very best I had to give. And now – well – I find I do not have much left to give.'

The man nodded but said nothing, so I went on:

'Since my new employer, Mr Farraday, arrived, I've tried very hard. But whatever I do, I find I'm making more and more errors

97

with my work. Unimportant errors, it's true, but I would never have made these errors in the past. And I know what these errors mean. I've given everything that I had to give. I gave it all to Lord Darlington.'

'Oh dear, do you want a handkerchief? I've got one somewhere,' my companion said.

'No thank you, it's quite all right. I'm very sorry. I'm afraid the travelling has made me tired. I'm very sorry.'

'You must have been very devoted to this Lord Darlington. And he died three years ago, you say?'

'Lord Darlington wasn't a bad man. He wasn't a bad man at all. At least he was able to say at the end of his life that he had made his own mistakes. His lordship was a courageous man. He chose a certain path in life. It proved to be a mistaken path, but at least he chose it for himself. I cannot claim that about myself. You see, I *trusted* in his lordship's wisdom. All those years I served him, I trusted that I was doing something worthwhile. I can't even say I made my own mistakes. Really – one has to ask oneself – where is the dignity in that?'

'Now look, I'm not sure I understand everything you're saying. But if you ask me, your attitude's all wrong, see? Don't keep looking back all the time, you'll only get depressed. Maybe you can't do your job as well as you used to, but it's the same for all of us. We've all got to relax at some time. Look at me – I've been very happy since I retired. We may not be as young as we were, but we have to keep looking forward.'

I believe it was then that he said:

'You've got to enjoy yourself. The evening's the best part of the day. You've done your day's work. Now you can relax and enjoy things. That's how I look at it. Ask anybody, they'll all tell you. The evening's the best part of the day.'

'I'm sure you're quite correct,' I said. 'I'm sorry. I'm probably too tired. I've been travelling rather a lot, you see.'

The man left twenty minutes ago, but I have remained here on this bench to witness the switching on of the pier lights. As I have already said, the happiness of the people around me at this small event seems to confirm what my companion said. For many people, the evening is the most enjoyable part of the day. Perhaps I should stop looking back so much. I should adopt a more positive attitude towards what remains of my day. After all, what purpose is there in forever looking back and blaming ourselves for what might or might not have happened? The hard reality, for people like you and me, is that our lives are in the hands of those great gentlemen who employ our services. What is the sense in worrying about whether we could or could not have taken more control? Surely it is enough that people like you and me have at least tried to make a real contribution, however small. Whatever the result is, surely that is a reason to be proud.

A few minutes ago, soon after the lights came on, I turned around on my bench and studied the crowd of people behind me. They were laughing and chatting. There are people of all ages wandering around this pier: families with children, couples, young and elderly, walking arm in arm. I paid particular attention to a group of six or seven people just a little way behind me. I thought at first that they were a group of friends. However, as I listened to their conversation, I realized that they were strangers who had never met before. As I watch them now, they are all laughing happily. It is strange how people can build such warmth among themselves so quickly. It is possible that these people are simply sharing the anticipation of the evening ahead. On the other hand, I think the warmth between them is probably more a result of their skill at bantering. I can hear them exchanging one bantering remark after another. Perhaps it is time for me to pay more serious attention to the subject of bantering. After all, when one thinks about it, it is not such a foolish thing to do – particularly if, for some reason, it contains the key to human warmth.

I have, of course, already spent much time practising my bantering skills. It is possible, however, that I need to be more enthusiastic about it. Perhaps, when I return to Darlington Hall tomorrow – Mr Farraday will be away for another week – I will make a new start. I shall start practising bantering again with new energy. If I do this, I shall be able to pleasantly surprise Mr Farraday with my new skill when he returns.

ACTIVITIES

Chapters 1–4

Before you read

1 Read the Introduction. Why is this story called *The Remains of the Day*?

2 Look at the Word List at the back of the book.
   a Which are words for people?
   b Which other words describe features of a large country house and gardens?
   c Would you like to work as a butler? Why (not)? What features of the job would you most / least enjoy?
   d Discuss which of these qualities are the most / least important for a successful butler. Why?
   intelligence   a sense of humour   ambition   sensitivity
   loyalty   a sense of curiosity and adventure
   a good speaking voice   dignity

While you read

3 Complete these sentences. Write one word in each space.
   a Stevens changes his mind about taking a break because he receives an unexpected ....
   b When Mr Farraday arrived, Darlington Hall had a staff of .... servants.
   c In the afternoon, Mr Farraday prefers .... to serious conversation.
   d Stevens feels that .... is a great butler's most important quality.
   e Stevens asked Miss Kenton not to use his .... first name.
   f Stevens's father accidentally left a .... outside the games room.
   g Lord Darlington told Stevens that he did not want any .... during the conference.
   h Stevens and his father rarely had .... with each other.

i Stevens's father was not happy about his list of new
....

j Lord Darlington believed that by 1920 .... had
suffered too much.

After you read

4 How does or did Stevens feel, and why,

   a when Mr Farraday invites him to take a break?

   b about his staff plan for Darlington Hall in 1956?

   c about bantering?

   d twenty minutes after he has left Darlington Hall?

   e about the English countryside?

   f about foreign butlers?

   g about Miss Kenton's attitude to his father?

   h about his father's mistakes?

   i about Lord Darlington?

   j about his own treatment of his father?

5 Work with another student. Have this conversation between
Stevens and Lord Darlington in 1922.

   Student A: You are Stevens. You want your father to work at
Darlington Hall. Tell Lord Darlington why your father
would be a better under-butler than many younger
men.

   Student B: You are Lord Darlington. You would prefer to employ
a younger man as a new under-butler. Tell Stevens
why.

6 Discuss these questions with another student.

   a Was Stevens right to be annoyed with Miss Kenton? Why
(not)?

   b Was Miss Kenton right to be annoyed with Stevens? Why
(not)?

   c Was Stevens a good son? Why (not)?

   d Was Lord Darlington a good employer? Why (not)?

   e Stevens says, 'It is not easy to find satisfactory staff nowadays.'
Why was it difficult at that time, do you think?

Chapters 5–8

Before you read

7 How do you think Stevens's father reacted to his new duties?

While you read

8 Who are these sentences about?

  a He was too embarrassed to speak to his
son about sex. ....

  b He misunderstood Stevens. ....

  c He had a bad leg. ....

  d He was ill on the first day of the conference. ....

  e He criticized Lord Darlington. ....

  f He was unaware that he was crying. ....

  g He was suspicious when he arrives at
Darlington Hall. ....

  h Stevens defended his reputation. ....

  i They lost their jobs. ....
and ....

  j He regretted an earlier decision. ....

After you read

9 What problems did these people cause for Stevens in this part of
the story?

  a his father **b** Monsieur Dupont **c** Miss Kenton

  d Lord Darlington

10 Whose words are these? Who were they speaking to, and in what
situation?

  a 'I would be grateful if, in future, you did not speak to me directly
at all.'

  b 'I know all about fish.'

  c 'I'm proud of you.'

  d 'Professionalism is just another word for greedy dishonesty.'

  e 'Will you permit me to close his eyes?'

  f 'Please don't think that I'm cold-hearted.'

  g 'The silver in this house is a delight.'

  h 'I will not work in a house in which such things can occur.'

    i 'I was a coward.'

    j 'Why, why, why do you always have to *pretend*?'

11 Discuss these questions with another student.

    a Was Stevens right to continue working while his father is dying? Why (not)?

    b Was Stevens right to obey Lord Darlington's request to dismiss the two housemaids? Why (not)?

    c Was Miss Kenton right not to have left Darlington Hall? Why (not)?

    d Who do you most agree with at the conference – Mr Lewis or Lord Darlington? Why?

Chapters 9–12

Before you read

12 How do you think that Stevens's relationship with Miss Kenton developed? Why?

While you read

13 Tick (✓) the correct answer.

    a When Lisa left Darlington Hall, Stevens felt

        1) sorry for Miss Kenton. .....

        2) angry with Lisa. .....

    b Stevens does not spend the night in Tavistock because

        1) he gets lost and runs out of petrol. .....

        2) the town is busier than he expected. .....

    c Stevens was annoyed with Miss Kenton because she wanted to

        1) brighten up his room. .....

        2) know what he was reading. .....

    d Stevens read love stories because he

        1) wanted to improve his vocabulary. .....

        2) secretly enjoyed romance and adventure. .....

    e Stevens was concerned about changes in Miss Kenton's

        1) levels of efficiency. .....

        2) general mood. .....

f Stevens would only be perfectly happy if
  1) Lord Darlington succeeded in his ambitions. .....
  2) he could stay at the highest level of his profession. .....
g Stevens ended the cocoa evenings because Miss Kenton
  1) seemed less and less interested in them. .....
  2) had not told him the truth about her leisure-time
     activities. .....
h Miss Kenton seemed confused and upset when Stevens
  1) discussed household matters with her. .....
  2) offered his condolences on her aunt's death. .....

After you read

14 How do you think Miss Kenton felt, and why,
  a after interviewing Lisa?
  b when Lisa left?
  c when Stevens tried to hide his book?
  d when Stevens asked her about her leisure-time activities?
  e when Stevens gave her his definition of contentment?
  f when Stevens commented on her increasing tiredness?
  g after Stevens stopped their evening discussions?
  h after her conversation with Stevens in the dining room?
15 Work with another student. Have this conversation.
  Student A: You are Miss Kenton. You are angry with Stevens
         after he has criticized you in the dining room (Chapter
         12). You think that he has treated you unfairly and
         been insensitive to you over the last few weeks. Tell
         him why.
  Student B: You are Stevens. You disagree with Miss Kenton. You
         think that you have treated her fairly and that she has
         no reason for complaint. Tell her why.
16 Discuss these questions with another student.
  a How many 'turning points' are there in Stevens's relationship
     with Miss Kenton in this part of the story?
  b Which of these turning points do you think is the most
     important? Why?

c How could Stevens have acted differently to avoid these turning points?

Chapters 13–15

Before you read

17 Discuss these questions with another student.

    a At the end of Chapter 12, Stevens uses the word 'dreams'. What dreams is he talking about? How do you think they were destroyed?

    b Have you ever experienced an embarrassing misunderstanding? How did it happen? How did you feel during and after it?

    c Have you ever met any famous people? Who were they? Where did you meet? Were they the same in real life as in your imagination?

While you read

18 Are these sentences true (✓) or false (✗)?

    a Miss Kenton said nothing in her letter about Darlington Hall.   .....

    b Mr and Mrs Taylor and their neighbours think that Stevens is a gentleman.   .....

    c The inhabitants of Moscombe have never met a gentleman before.   .....

    d Stevens enjoys deceiving the villagers.   .....

    e Mr Spencer and Lord Darlington agreed that democracy was old-fashioned.   .....

    f Stevens thinks that important decisions should only be taken by great gentlemen like Lord Darlington.   .....

    g Dr Carlisle is surprised when Stevens admits that he is really a butler.   .....

    h While he is waiting to meet Miss Kenton in Little Compton, Stevens spends all morning thinking about Lord Darlington.   .....

19 Answer these questions.

Why:

a do the villagers believe that Stevens is a gentleman?

b doesn't Stevens tell the villagers the truth about himself?

c did Mr Spencer ask Stevens three questions?

d did Lord Darlington talk to Stevens about a 'house on fire'?

What:

e does Stevens want to find out when he meets Miss Kenton?

f is a gentleman's greatest quality, according to Stevens?

g does Stevens think of Harry Smith's political opinions?

How:

h did Lord Darlington feel about Mr Spencer's treatment of Stevens?

i does Dr Carlisle know that Stevens is probably a butler?

j does Dr Carlisle feel about the previous evening's misunderstanding?

20 Work with another student. Have this conversation between two voters during a general election.

Student A: You intend to vote for Harry Smith as your local Member of Parliament. Tell the other voter why.

Student B: You think that Mr Spencer would be a better Member of Parliament. Tell the other voter why.

21 Discuss these questions with another student.

a Stevens says, 'It was my duty to be loyal to him [Lord Darlington], and not to worry about whether he was right or wrong.' Do you agree that this was his duty? Why (not)?

b If you were Dr Carlisle, would you tell the villagers the truth about Stevens? Why (not)?

Chapters 16–18

Before you read

22 How will the story end for Stevens and Miss Kenton, do you think? Why?

23 Find the correct endings, below, to these sentences.

    a Mr Cardinal visited Lord Darlington because he …

    b Mr Cardinal frequently visited Darlington Hall, although Lord Darlington …

    c Miss Kenton was angry with Stevens because she …

    d Mr Cardinal thought that Stevens …

    e Stevens was not shocked, although Lord Darlington …

    f Stevens did not comfort Miss Kenton because he …

    g Stevens felt proud of himself because he …

    h Lord Darlington was unpopular after the war because he …

    i Stevens suspects that he …

    j Stevens thinks he might be happier if he …

    1) was too busy.

    2) has exaggerated the importance of dignity.

    3) thought that he was blind to his own feelings.

    4) wanted the King of England to visit Germany.

    5) had survived a difficult evening with dignity.

    6) learns how to banter.

    7) was considered to have betrayed his country.

    8) disagreed with his political views.

    9) showed too little curiosity in world affairs.

    10) wanted some information.

After you read

24 Discuss these questions with another student.

    a Why does Stevens feel that 'his heart was breaking' (Chapter 17)?

    b Which is

      1) the saddest

      2) the most amusing

      3) the most surprising

    part of the story? Why?

Writing

25 Imagine that you are Stevens. Write a reply to Miss Kenton's letter (Chapter 1). Tell her about life with Mr Farraday, and your plans to visit her in September.

26 Imagine that you are young Mr Cardinal (Chapter 6). Write a letter to your future wife, describing Lord Darlington's conference and Stevens's strange behaviour. Why do *you* think Stevens was so keen to talk to you about the 'beauty of nature'?

27 Miss Kenton says to Stevens, 'Why do you always have to *pretend*?' (Chapter 8) Describe three examples of Stevens's inability to express his feelings honestly. How would things have been different if he *had* been able to express himself properly on these occasions?

28 'Stevens accidentally hurts a lot of people, but the biggest victim is himself.' Do you agree with this statement? Why (not)?

29 Imagine that you are Stevens. After Miss Kenton leaves Darlington Hall, write an advertisement for a new housekeeper. Describe the duties, and the type of person you are looking for. How would the right person find this a particularly rewarding job?

30 Imagine that you are young Mr Cardinal. Write an article for your newspaper about Lord Darlington. Describe why you think he is an honourable but foolish man.

31 Imagine that you are Miss Kenton. Write a letter to a friend about Stevens, from Darlington Hall. Describe his character and your feelings about him. Include one or two 'amusing little stories' about him.

32 Stevens says (Chapter 18), 'We have to leave the big decisions of life to those great gentlemen who employ our services.' Is he right? Why (not)? Write an article about it.

33 Imagine that you are Stevens. Write a letter (in his style, as much as possible) to Mr Farraday in America. Thank him for the use of his car and describe your journey to the West Country.

34 Write a paragraph about the importance of these people in the story. What do we learn about Stevens's character from them? Stevens's father   Sarah and Ruth   the villagers of Moscombe

WORD LIST

affection (n) a feeling of liking or love, and caring

anticipation (n) expectation that something is going to happen

banter (n/v) friendly conversation with shared jokes and amusing remarks about each other

butler (n) the most senior male servant in a house

climax (n) the most important part of a story or situation, usually near the end

cocoa (n) a sweet hot drink made from sugar, milk or water, and a brown powder from the beans that are used to make chocolate

condolences (n pl) sympathetic feelings for someone whose relative or friend has died

devoted (adj) giving love, attention or strong support

dignity (n) the ability to behave in a calm, controlled way even in a difficult situation

drawing room (n) a room, especially in a large house, where you can entertain guests or relax

fair (n) an event at which people show and sell products

footman (n) a male servant, in the past, whose duties included opening the door and announcing the names of visitors

for (conj) a formal word meaning 'because'

grounds (n pl) the land or gardens surrounding a large building

indeed (adv) a word used to emphasize a statement or to introduce an additional statement that supports what you have just said

landing (n) the floor at the top of a staircase, or between two sets of stairs

landlady (n) a woman who rents rooms to people

lawn (n) an area of ground in a garden that is covered in short grass

maid (n) a female servant

nostalgia (n) a feeling that a time in the past was good

pier (n) a long, large walkway that is built out over the sea

prime minister (n) the leader of the government in many countries that have a parliament

puppet (n) a person controlled by other people, who make decisions for them

refreshments (n pl) small amounts of food and drink

senator (n) a member of the Senate, one of the two groups of people who make the laws in the United States

stroke (n) a medical condition in which a vein bursts or is blocked in your brain, causing death or the inability to use some muscles

summerhouse (n) a small building in the garden, where people sit in warm weather

tray (n) a flat piece of metal, plastic or wood, with raised edges, used for carrying food or drink

trolley (n) a small table on wheels for serving food or carrying equipment

turning point (n) the beginning of an important change, especially of an improvement in a situation

Schindler's List
Thomas Keneally

Thomas Keneally's famous novel tells the true story of Oskar Schindler, a businessman who risked his life every day during the Second World War to save as many Jews as possible. Steven Spielberg's film of *Schindler's List* won seven Oscars, including Best Picture and Best Director.

North and South
Elizabeth Gaskell

Life changes completely for Margaret Hale and her parents when they move to a smoky northern city. There, Margaret meets Mr Thornton, a wealthy cotton mill owner, and dislikes him immediately. But the mill owner falls passionately in love with her. Then his workers strike. Against a background of industrial drama and personal tragedy, is there any hope for Mr Thornton's dream?

Man from the South and Other Stories
Roald Dahl

Roald Dahl is the master of the unexpected. Things are not always what they seem and nobody should be trusted. In this collection of his short stories we learn some strange lessons about the dangerous world we live in. But you will have to wait until the final pages of each story to discover the last, terrible twist!

There are hundreds of Penguin Readers to choose from – world classics, film adaptations, modern-day crime and adventure, short stories, biographies, American classics, non-fiction, plays ...

For a complete list of all Penguin Readers titles, please contact your local Pearson Longman office or visit our website.